Born and brought up in Sussex, Tess Stimson read English Literature at St Hilda's College, Oxford, before spending a number of years as a news producer with ITN, travelling to war-zones and hotspots all over the globe. She is now a full-time writer and journalist, writing regularly for the *Daily Mail* and several women's magazines. She is the author of one biography and six novels, including the bestselling *The Adultery Club*, *The Infidelity Chain* and *The Cradle Snatcher*. She lives in Vermont with her American husband, Erik, their daughter, Lily, and her two sons, Henry and Matthew.

www.tessstimson.com

Also by Tess Stimson

Yours Till the End
Hard News
Soft Focus
Pole Position
The Adultery Club
The Infidelity Chain
The Cradle Snatcher

Beat the Bitch

How to stop the other woman stealing your man

Tess Stimson

MACMILLAN

First published 2009 by Macmillan
an imprint of Pan Macmillan Ltd
Pan Macmillan, 20 New Wharf Road, London N1 9RR
Basingstoke and Oxford
Associated companies throughout the world
www.panmacmillan.com

ISBN 978-0-230-71452-6

A CIP catalogue record for this book is available
from the British Library.

Printed and bound in the UK by
CPI Mackays, Chatham ME5 8TD

Visit **www.panmacmillan.com** to read more about all our books
and to buy them. You will also find features, author interviews and
news of any author events, and you can sign up for e-newsletters
so that you're always first to hear about our new releases.

For the girls
(in strict alphabetical order):
Danusia, Georgie, Michèle and Sarah –
couldn't have done it without you!

The Crimewatch Caveat

Please remember that while frightening things do happen, the chances they will happen to you are still relatively small. This book is intended as a guide in the unlikely event you find yourself a victim of a love crime. However, it should in no way be used as a substitute for your own common sense. There may well be a perfectly innocent explanation for the naked woman in bed with your man, especially if he has a pink feather duster stuck up his bottom, and it should be considered carefully in context before reaching a conclusion. (Please note: cutting off his willy with a kitchen knife is still illegal, and makes a dreadful mess on the sheets. The author neither recommends nor advocates physical abuse. You can do more than enough with verbal, especially if you mention his mother.)

All anecdotes and examples in this book are true. However, some names have been changed to protect the guilty.

Don't have nightmares; do sleep well.

Contents

Beat the Bitch

Chapter One
Why You Need to Read This Book

There's an old saying that goes men need only four things in life: food, shelter, pussy – and *new* pussy.

Frankly, it paints the XY gender as sophisticates.

Take four men propping up a bar. Four men in committed relationships (either married, or living with a woman who, touchingly, thinks she's as good as) from four different walks of life. A teacher, perhaps, and an accountant. A builder and a physiotherapist. It doesn't really matter what they do. Three of them will always have one thing in common.

They're screwing around.

Maybe not all of them right now, today. But yes, *three out of four men* have cheated, or will cheat, on their wives and/or girlfriends.

That's a monumentally depressing statistic. Only *one* of our charming barflies will actually manage to keep his trousers zipped. Are you sure that freakishly faithful fellow is *your* man?

Loyal as a hound? OK, try this curve-ball. More than two-thirds of wives and/or girlfriends whose men cat around *have no idea their man is cheating*. Yes, it's official: you *will* be the last to know.

Unless you read this book, of course.

As the great Pat Benatar put it, love is a battlefield. You may think as you finally emerge from the romantic combat zone with Mr (Oh, All) Right – and Christ, the *relief* of making it safely through no-straight-man's land, a.k.a. dating after the age of thirty – that the war is finally over.

Oh, you dear, sweet child. The war is only just *beginning*.

Until now, you've had one thing in your favour. You probably aren't the dirtiest woman he's had in bed (your mother was right: men never *marry* those sorts of girls) or the sexiest woman he's ever dated. He's probably seen better tits and perkier arses. But at least you had *novelty*.

Now, however, the ring is on your finger (or at least your pink toothbrush is nuzzling his blue toothbrush), and you aren't as new as you once were. In fact, you're dangerously close to becoming . . . well, *old* pussy.

Somewhere out there, a scheming Bitch who can't be bothered to train her own man to put the seat back down has set her sights on *yours*.

She may not be younger. She may not be prettier (Princess Diana and Camilla Parker Bowles, anyone?). But she's ruthless.

Is your relationship Bitch-proof?

- Do you still give him blow-jobs? Seriously, not ever?
- Do you know the name of his boss and at least three of his work colleagues?
- Do you know exactly what he does at work (other than update his Facebook entry/look at porn?)
- Do you tell him he's wonderful and sexy every day (as opposed to muttering 'Bloody wanker' under your breath every five minutes)?
- Do you book bedroom time with each other, or do you prefer to 'make love spontaneously' (i.e. when he finally goes on and on about not getting it for so bloody long you give in just for a quiet life)?
- Do you stop what you're doing, switch off *The X Factor*, and kiss him when he gets in from work?
- Do you ever argue (or have you given up trying to get him to see things your way)?
- Do you pee in front of him?
- Do you even own a pair of stockings any more?
- Do you talk him up to your friends, or do you spend all your time bitching about him?
- Do you spend time thinking how to please him, or are you too busy thinking of ways he doesn't please you?

'Why should you feel guilty, mistresses?'

Look, girls, let me be straight: it's a jungle out there. Life is bloody difficult: we all struggle every day to juggle work and relationships and kids and pornographic fantasies about Daniel Craig. Men are no help at all, but we *expect* that. What we shouldn't have to deal with are Trojan Horse attacks from inside our own ranks.

A few quick examples: a recent issue of *Cosmopolitan* offered 'Cougar Skills to Crib', tips from 'babes who've been around the block' to reel in a man. Yours or someone else's, they didn't seem particularly fussy.

As I wrote this, yet another dating website for married men who want to play away discreetly was launched – *by women* – and then crashed under the deluge of single women wanting to sign on.

Type the word 'affair' into Amazon and a slurry (I use the word advisedly) of how-to-cheat titles appears: *Have Your Cake and Eat It*; *Love Tactics: How to Win the One You Want*; *Sinful Sex*; *Having an Affair: A Handbook for the Other Woman*.

'Why should you feel guilty, mistresses?' asks the author of this last title. 'There's no need. It's not your fault, after all.'

Being a mistress used to be a shameful, shabby secret. No longer. There's a new breed of women out there who believe in taking what, and *who*, they want. (Who knows, maybe you were one of them once. I'll admit I was; how else do you think I know what the Bitches are up to?)

Some women actually prefer married men. 'They're

already house-trained,' as one mistress put it to me recently. 'They know the importance of jewellery, and they're *grateful*.'

Let's face it, seducing a man is pitifully easily. The truth of the matter is that (to borrow from Oscar Wilde, who knew a bit about it) men can resist everything except temptation.

Penicillin has a lot to answer for

This is not to denigrate *all* men, of course – after all, a magnificent one in four does manage to keep his pants on – it's merely to accept the way things are. Like it or not (and this is *no excuse*), men are not naturally monogamous. Five hundred years ago, few marriages lasted longer than a decade, mainly because either he died in battle, or she died giving birth. Frankly, no one had *time* to get bored.

These days, in lieu of a sword through the gullet or raging septicaemia, we have the mid-life crisis and divorce. Penicillin has a lot to answer for.

If you've bothered to read this far, you've *de facto* acknowledged that there is perhaps a teeny, tiny *possibility* that another woman might be making the moves on your man. Carry on reading, and you'll find out how to slap the Bitch down before it gets out of hand.

I know what I'm talking about. In my twenties, like so many of my friends, I didn't stop and think to ask if the men I dated were free or not. As far as I was concerned, if a man already had someone scraping his ruined dinner into the bin/dog at home, *he* was the one cheating, not me. When I fell in love with a married man, I ruthlessly played a high-stakes game, and won. It would have been so easy for his wife to beat me, however, if she'd known a few simple rules.

Rules I'm going to share with you.

Poacher turned gamekeeper

Eight years after we married, I got careless. And, yes, a little tired of attending to the needs of my high-maintenance alpha-male husband. Another woman (later wife no. 4) scented blood in the water and swooped in, stealing my moves and my man. It was no more than I deserved: the great cosmic karma credit plan.

I could have marshalled my forces and staged a counter-coup. But at the time I was too distraught to think clearly. And whilst there are plenty of books telling you *how* to have an affair, and even more offering to help you recover *after* one, there are none explaining how to stop a predatory Bitch from stealing your man in the first place.

(Oh yes, and let's get one favourite Bitch excuse out of the way here and now. 'You can't steal a man,' they whine defensively, 'they're not suitcases. They choose who they want to be with.' Yes, and I'm the Virgin Mary. We all know any woman can lead a man by the nose – or by a rather lower portion of his anatomy – if she's a mind. And a short skirt. Men are stupid, but women are cold-blooded and unscrupulous. We all know who's *really* to blame.)

So here's the book I wish I'd had when it mattered. Poacher turned gamekeeper, that's me. I'll arm you with the knowledge to spot and terminate an affair as soon as – preferably before – it happens.

By the time you're done, he'll be begging you to take him back. The only question you'll have left to decide is

Do you want to?

In a nutshell

This book will give you:

Red alert: the signs he's cheating

The low-down on the lie-down: seduction tricks she uses to drive your man wild in bed

Tips direct from the horse's mouth: from the trollops sleeping with your men

Insights from the Infidels: from the men whose wills prove so much weaker than their willies

How to screw him in the event of divorce: naughty insider info from some of the country's top divorce lawyers

Revenge tips: helpful suggestions for sweet vengeance that won't land you in jail

If, after everything, you decide you want to keep him, I'll tell you how to do it. You may not like everything I say, but I promise it'll work.

Chapter Two
Know Thy Enemy

That whole 'sisters are doing it for themselves' thing? That's not a girl-power anthem; it's a *threat*.

I hope you're getting the picture by now. Even if you're 100 per cent certain your man isn't having an affair (*really? Given all I've just told you?*), that doesn't mean he isn't being stalked by a posse of twenty-two-year-old babes even as we speak.

When women go to war, they take no prisoners and show no mercy. It's an evolution thing: back in *Jurassic Park* days (yes, yes, OK, I know Homo sapiens didn't co-exist with the dinosaurs; cut me some slack), the men went off hunting together and had to watch out for each other if they didn't want to become a sabre-toothed tiger's breakfast. There's a lot of male bonding goes on when you're all stuck up a tree with a very pissed-off woolly mammoth pacing around underneath.

But you couldn't trust a *woman* with one of those nasty, pointy spear things. They could take someone's eye out! Women aren't designed to go hunting; look at how their right breasts keep getting in the way of their bow arm. Far better to leave all that dangerous, exciting hunting stuff to the boys.

Never mind that women wouldn't have got lost in the primordial swamp for weeks at a time, but would have stopped to ask one of those nice Neanderthals the way back to the caves. Women wouldn't have left it to the last minute to go hunting, and missed all the best buffalo. No, if women had been in charge, they'd have dropped out of the trees, discovered fire, invented the wheel, the combustion engine and a really *good* hair remover, and knocked out Stonehenge, all before you could say ten million years BC.

However, men got the penises and the small brains. So women had to make do with sitting around the campfire complimenting each other on that nice new shade of woad, and plotting how to stab each other in the back with a sharpened mastodon tooth.

A sweet nook for some sweet nookie

'Wait a minute. What about all the girly camaraderie?' I hear you ask. After all, the women got to spend all day together too, stirring the pot, waiting for the boys to come home. It must have been just like a sleepover, really: trying on each other's tigerskin hot-pants, painting each other's noses with river mud, gossiping about who's doing what to whom in the latest episode of cave-drawing.

OK. First, have you ever *been* to a sleepover? It's like a cross between bear-baiting and bull-fighting, only not as good-natured. Five teenage girls could eat Ghenghis Khan for breakfast.

Second, the law of the jungle – survival of the fittest – meant it was just never going to work that way. Think about it. The men got first pick of the juiciest cuts of roast mammoth. They got the fluffiest pile of furs to sleep on, the least draughty nooks of the cave, because they were bigger and stronger than the women. And the best of everything always went to the man highest up the food chain. If a girl fancied a delicate morsel of dried terrapin, say, or a cosy spot by the fire, she had to sweet-talk a man – preferably the alpha male – into giving it to her. Hardly a problem: men have always been happy to exchange a sweet nook for some sweet nookie. No, her only real challenge came from the *other women* who wanted to be Mrs Alpha too.

Until the late twentieth century, with a few notable exceptions (Boudicca comes to mind, or those scary Amazons who hacked off that inconvenient right breast), a woman was totally reliant on her ability to partner up with, or manipulate, a man to get ahead. She had absolutely no power, no control, no independence of her own. A woman had to curb her tongue, suppress her desires and kowtow to her husband, even when she knew best (which was obviously pretty much all the time).

Hard for us to get our sweet little enfranchised heads around now, but back in the day, as a woman you owned nothing. Not even your own body. Once you married, your husband had the *right* to have sex with you whenever he wanted. Foreplay? *Orgasms?* Get real. You weren't even allowed to say no.

(Incidentally, in the Victorian age, women suffering from faintness, insomnia, irritability, loss of appetite or a 'tendency to cause trouble' (i.e. have an opinion) were carted off to doctors who gave them an internal 'pelvic massage' until their patients experienced 'hysterical paroxysm'. Unsurprisingly, this treatment proved extremely popular. When the poor put-upon medics complained their hands were getting tired, some bright spark invented a clockwork 'massage device' to do the hard work, and hey presto! the vibrator was born. These quacks were paid to bring women off. Seriously. I think I would have been troublesome very frequently!

Dried-up virgin

So, anyway. If a girl wanted any kind of life, other than looking after her aged parents and dying a childless dried-up virgin, she had to net herself a bloke. Preferably a sane, presentable, solvent one younger than her own grandfather.

If she failed to land a decent catch, she could be married off to an unfaithful loser, and there was nothing she could do about it (other than visit that nice doctor rather a lot). She couldn't leave him, unless she wanted to end up destitute. Everything she brought to him on marriage, everything she inherited during that marriage, belonged to him, including her children. If he screwed things up – lost the house, gambled the money away, disinherited the children – she could do nothing about it. She could be brilliant and intelligent herself, but if she was married to a wanker then she was for ever Mrs Wanker, like it or not.

Little wonder snaring a good husband was so vitally important. Which brings us to why women are such ruthless, immoral, man-stealing Bitches.

> 'Solvent, successful, good-looking men are rarely single. It's like handbags: you always want the must-have clutch everyone's fighting over, not the cheap, ugly handbag sitting on the shelf. I don't have a problem if he's married or living with someone. This is real life, not a polite game of croquet. There are no "rules".'
>
> *Greta, 32, marketing executive*

Yes, of course men have affairs with other chaps' girls too; but they usually feel jolly rotten about it. Chances are, if two men discover they're making whoopee with the same woman, they'll both dump her and go down the pub for a drink to drown their sorrows. Before long they'll be best mates, going off on fishing trips together and naming their first-borns after each other.

Where did all the good men go?

But with women, there's no honour among thieves. Millennia of pouting, batting eyelashes, acting dumb and reeling in a man can't be wiped out in a few decades of feminism. We no longer need a man to finance and support us, but the competitive instinct runs deep.

And like it or not, the new age of female independence has brought its own problems. For successful, career-orientated women, there is *still* a dearth of sane, presentable, solvent men out there. Because while we are off getting PhDs, finding power jobs and putting our Manolos on the first rung of the ladder, our not-so-dumb sisters are out there pouting and batting their eyelashes like their great-great-grandmas before them. By the time we hit thirty and look around for a nice man to share our penthouses and BMW Z4s and give us children, *all the men are gone*.

My daughter is six, and sparklingly bright. And when she's a little older, I shall tell her this: 'Go to university, get your degree, and have the time of your life. And then put your career to one side for a while, find a decent man and have your children before you reach thirty.' With her brains and a good education, she won't have any problem rebuilding a career later, her home and family secure behind her.

But concentrate on the career first, and expect the man to slot into place when you're good and ready, and you'll probably end up unhappy and alone.

OK, throw this book across the room if you like. Heresy, I know. But I'm only telling it like it is. And I hope you pick it up again and read on, because, trust me, you *really* need to.

So what do all those thirty-something career women do when they find out there's a supply shortage and all the good men are taken? Why, *they steal one*, of course.

The sandwich girl

Some women are simply addicted to seduction: to the high of reeling in a man. Maybe they have self-esteem issues; Daddy didn't tell them they were beautiful enough when they were little. Maybe they were always the last at school to be picked for the netball team. Maybe they're just selfish little cows. Who cares? This isn't about *understanding*

Bitches. It's about sending them scuttling back under the rocks they slithered out from.

For these sad slappers who get off on getting off, what better hit than a *married* man? There's the added buzz of not just getting a man into bed, but having him climb (metaphorically, unless you're moving in circles that are a little beyond the scope of this book) over his wife or girl-friend to get to you.

(Note to any Bitches reading this: this is in fact crap reasoning on your part, since married men are the easiest to seduce, on account of their weak wills. And self-governing willies. Put it this way: men give their penis a name for one reason only – so that they don't have a total stranger making all their decisions for them.)

An interesting corollary to the above: women whose men have dumped them for another woman (especially publicly) often go out and steal a man themselves. It's as if they've been so hurt and humiliated by what's happened, the only way to feel better about themselves is to prove they can snare a 'taken' man too.

> 'Simon walked out on me two weeks before our ninth wedding anniversary, for the girl who delivered sand-wiches to his office. The sandwich girl! She was ten years younger than me, but not particularly slim or pretty. I deliberately started an affair with the husband of a woman I knew slightly, just to prove I still had what it took. It need-ed to be a married man, I don't know why. I'm not proud of it, but it made me feel good about myself again. And at least I made sure she never found out.'
>
> *Amanda, 34, IT consultant*

Blame it on evolution. A dearth of decent men. The way your mother put your hat on. The favourite Bitch excuse that I ran across in the course of my research, both informal (friends, a bottle of Sauvignon and a box of tissues) and formal (notebook, telephone, cold coffee) is still the old 'I fell in love' lament. Though I'm really not buying this one. Bitches, I've been there, and I can tell you there's always a point at which you *can* help it, and *choose* not to.

The slapper's tale

OK, this is the bit where I come clean and 'fess up. Frankly, I'd rather airbrush my personal history and remove all the dodgy bits (and, in fact, have frequently done so for my mother's benefit), but for you I'll stand up like a woman and put it out there so you can learn from my less-than-reputable reputation.

When I met my first husband, he was already married to someone else. I knew this, since we worked for the same company, but the 'word on the street' was that he and his wife had separated recently, a rumour he confirmed when we met by chance at a party. So far, so what – right?

Oh, darling, *no*.

We hooked up, and with the carelessness of youth I didn't trouble to probe further. Divorced, separated, what did it matter? It was just a technicality. He was basically a free agent, wasn't he?

Putting aside the fact that it's *never* a good idea to get involved with a man until the dust has well and truly settled on his previous relationship (oh the baggage! Oh the tears and turmoil and the to-ing and fro-ing!), he was *not*, in fact, a free agent. His wife was abroad doing her own thing at the time, yes, but she fully expected to come back to her husband (and two-year-old daughter . . . yes, there was a child, and no, I'm ashamed to admit it made no difference to me) and pick up her marriage where she'd left off.

Clearly there were problems with this geographically challenged relationship before I appeared on the scene. But I hardly helped, now, did I?

He assured me the marriage was over. However, he added, he'd recently signed a contract with one of those puritanical, holier-than-thou American companies, and was nervous they'd cancel it if he dumped his wife and ran off with a floozie (yes, that would be me) barely half his age. He needed to . . . how shall we put it? . . . finesse the split a little. Which meant he would temporarily return to his wife . . . but of course he *really* loved *me*.

If a friend came to me with a tale like this, I'd slap her upside the head and tell her to run a bloody mile. 'He's spinning you a line!' I'd storm. 'This is total bullshit! *Married men never leave their wives.*'

And indeed, that might have been the end of it – had his wife not totally mishandled things when she found out.

She had a golden opportunity to kick me into touch. She held (almost) all the cards: the natural home advantage of the incumbent; a beautiful baby daughter he adored; and, thanks to the judgemental Americans, his career in the palm of her hand; plus he'd already been divorced once before (oh, didn't I mention that bit?) and knew precisely how hard, expensive and miserable an experience it was.

Meanwhile, I was on the other side of the world (affairs

need means and opportunity, as well as motive) and hardly in a position to call the shots and do what needed to be done (Oral! Oral! Oral!) to secure him.

What she should have done – assuming she wanted to stay married to him, of course – was seduce him back again. With a bit of calm, considered, intelligent TLC, which was all the poor man was really looking for, she'd have seen me off in an instant.

What she absolutely, categorically, emphatically *shouldn't* have done was 'smack him around the face' (as she told the *Daily Express* later) and then march into the five-star hotel room where he and I had snatched a weekend together, drag him bodily from the hotel in front of an enthralled audience and, according to him, keep up the rant for approximately three weeks without drawing breath.

But she didn't have the benefit of this book (specifically Chapter Eight: What *Not* to Do). And who feels calm or considered when they've just found out their husband is getting his end away elsewhere?

Men have tender egos. They don't like being humiliated or made to feel in the wrong, even when they've crossed the line so long ago that it's a tiny dot receding into the distance.

It really wasn't difficult for me to employ a few favourite Bitch tricks and win the day. Wives, you have been warned.

Bitch tricks

1. Laugh at all his jokes as if he's the funniest man alive
2. Compliment him at least three times per twenty-minute conversation
3. Always be available for sex; initiate it whenever possible
4. Always dress up for him, especially in the bedroom
5. Entertain him, but make sure he's always the focus of attention; the conversation should always be about him
6. Never discuss your problems
7. Hang on his words. Make it clear you look up to him. Be impressed
8. Subtly imply his wife doesn't appreciate him, isn't good enough for him and is rather too keen on spending his money (never attack her directly – he'll get defensive)
9. Be a constant presence. Talk and text often – preferably dirty. Tell him what you want to do to him next time you meet
10. Find out what he used to love doing when he was young – and have him do it again with you

(Note to the morally outraged: I got my come-uppance, as you'll find out later in this book. Eight years after we met, I discovered he was cheating on *me*. So, did I learn my lesson from my predecessor and respond accordingly? Did I hell. Though I *did* have a rather more lucrative divorce than she did – see Chapter Twelve: Don't Get Mad, Get Diamonds.)

'Get something for yourself'

It's no defence, but I was deeply in love with the man. Back then, I thought that made a difference. And I did truly believe his marriage was already over. But I accept that none of this excuses my behaviour. *At all.*

Love's tricky. We've all done stupid and reprehensible things when in its thrall. But some Bitches don't even bother with that fig leaf of an excuse.

Remember that charming book I mentioned in the first chapter? *Having an Affair: A Handbook for Bitches* – sorry – *the 'Other Woman'*? This isn't a tome for those unlucky enough to fall in love with a man who happens to be married (which does happen, of course, especially when the bastards take their wedding rings off and then lie through their teeth). No, this is a cold, cynical manual for women who ruthlessly set out to elbow their way into another woman's relationship, primarily for material gain.

Its author, the delightful Ms Symonds, is robustly upfront. 'Make sure you're getting something of quality out of your affair,' she instructs her aspirational trollops.

'Even if it's 'only' great sex, a promotion at work, or a bit of help with the deposit on that new car, get something for yourself, *please.*'

'You should embrace any and every opportunity to live the high life with him, and through him, enjoying the gifts, sex, passion and travel that may – and in fact *should* – come your way!'

(One could argue there's a word for women who receive remuneration for activity in the bedroom. And it's not 'chambermaid'.)

This grubby candour does us one favour, however. Know thy enemy, after all. The good news is there's little new information in this rather predictable, banal book.

The bad news is that an awful lot of men are predictable and banal too.

Tying knots in cherry stalks

Let's see, what insightful gems does this self-proclaimed 'professional mistress' offer? Well, first she tells us that the main reason men stray is lack of sex. No shit, Sherlock. There are many reasons men screw around (of which more later) but it doesn't take a neuroscientist to work out that if it was just about being pampered, petted and being told they're the centre of the universe around which all else revolves, they'd go home to Mother.

What so many women fail to realize is that men are hard-wired to want sex. We expect men to put up with our hormonal roller-coaster moods and need for understanding and affection because we can't help it, it's the way we were made. But men were made to want sex. *A lot.* Why are their needs less valid?

So, surprise, surprise: Bitches offer sex. (Who'd have thought?) More sex; *new pussy* sex. And – at least in the beginning – it's also easy, carefree, no-strings sex that comes without baggage or history or a whole slew of tit-for-tat grievances.

Plus, it's *honeymoon sex*. You know, the kind of sex you only have at the beginning of a relationship. And an affair, because of its bite-size, tantalizing nature, effectively extends the 'beginning' pretty much indefinitely.

But when it comes down to it, it's not really about tying knots in cherry stalks with your tongue or swinging from a trapeze (though for those of you with an athletic bent and an open mind, check out Chapter Eleven: Ten Things Men Really Like in Bed).

(Note to the gossip-minded: a prominent politician who shall remain nameless told me the true story of a celebrated high-class call-girl, whose *pièce de resistance* involved a trapeze. Apparently, while he was stretched out naked on her bed, she climbed on the trapeze and twisted the chains round and round, like kids do at the swings. She then lowered herself on to his cock, raised her legs, and let go. Round and round she went on his dick, round and round . . .)

What women often forget is that sex is to a husband what conversation is to a wife. Imagine if he refused to talk to you for a week. A month. God help us, a *year*. You'd call him cruel and abusive, and you'd be right. But every time you slap his hand away and turn him down, you're treating him in exactly the same way. Little wonder, then, if he goes off to find someone else to 'talk' to.

Oral! Oral! Oral!

Whilst I'm sure they'd appreciate trapeze action, all most men are really looking for is a little bit of willingness and enthusiasm in the bedroom; and, with luck, the kind of energetic, appreciative performance you put in during the early days, when you were up for anything.

According to one call-girl I interviewed, oral sex is number one on her most requested list; and number one on the list of things wives and girlfriends *stop* doing once they're safely settled in the relationship.

Contrary to the myth of the quick and dirty fumble against a wall, 'The clients I see like a leisurely encounter,' she explained. 'The wife is too busy, tired or stressed for anything other than quickie sex, if that, and [my clients] want a slow seduction, with foreplay, pre- and post-coital cuddles, and all those things they had with their lover before they married.'

> 'Never make the mistake of thinking that an affair is just about sex. Visiting a prostitute is about sex, but an affair, like the relationship between courtesan and client, is based on intimacy on a multitude of levels. Understanding the mind and what arouses it is part of understanding what excites the body.'
>
> **The English Courtesan,**
> **www.englishcourtesan.blogspot.com**

OK, girls. Hands up. Sound like you?

Your husband doesn't expect you to look like Claudia Schiffer (unless you *are* Claudia Schiffer). As long as you don't morph into a shell-suited lard mountain, he won't even notice that extra ten pounds. It's got to be an ego-boost that he fancies you and wants to have sex with you despite your cellulite and stretch marks and kit-bag boobs. So why aren't you biting his bloody hand off?

Most people expect monogamy in marriage, not celibacy. Yes, you're more tired now. Yes, you may have a demanding job, and/or kids, or a secret life as a vampire. But *his needs haven't changed.*

It's great that you clean the house and cook a mean lasagne. Marvellous that you're a kick-ass CEO who still finds time to run Brownies and orchestrate the school Spring Benefit Ball. He's just thrilled that you're happy to get up at six to run little Johnny to footie practice on the other side of town, throw a dinner party for fifty, plant 200 narcissi and hand-paint hard-boiled Easter eggs for Susie's entire nursery-school class. But he could hire someone else to do most of those jobs (and, to be frank, he doesn't really give a stuff about the hand-painted eggs). One assumes you don't want him to hire someone to take care of the bedroom side of things.

I don't know about you, but I really enjoy sex. It's free, it's warming, and what's not to like about multiple orgasms? Even if I'm not in the mood to begin with, once we get going and the pump is primed, as it were, I light up like a Christmas tree. My husband is jolly good at the whole business, and would put his best foot forward every night if he could. And yet . . . and yet (oh, the shame!) there have been times I'd do almost anything to get out of it.

Me: 'Look, could we give it a miss tonight? I've got: (a) a really bad headache/backache/ingrown toenail; (b) a highly infectious cold; (c) a scary publisher and an overdue manuscript; (d) my period [the poor bugger must think women menstruate once a fortnight for at least ten days]; (e) your mother on the phone.

Him: Sigh.

Yes, I admit it: sewing in name-tapes (a torture akin to electrodes on your nipples) has occasionally ranked higher on the To Do list than dynamite sex with a man I adored.

The thing is, by the time I'd walked the kids a mile to school, crammed ten hours' writing into six, done the laundry, hit the supermarket, collected the kids from school (and I swear it was five miles the second time), cooked dinner, practised spelling, helped with fractions, advised on science projects, chivvied through bathtime, collapsed in front of *House*, poured a G&T and had a bath myself, the idea of swinging from the chandeliers (or, frankly, even staying conscious) was beyond me. When, on occasion, I was gently reminded that it had been three weeks/three months/the last time I got into your knickers England won the World Cup, and sweet-talked into a quickie, I'd watch the clock over his shoulder and think, *But I have to be up again in six hours!* Not really conducive to orgasmic ecstasy, however diligently your husband tongues your clitoris.

With a schedule like this, of course I was too tired. OK, the kids had to be fed and watered, but if sex is on the menu, it's amazing how keen a man can be to fold laundry or battle through four pages of algebra.

Girls these days think that using their feminine wiles to smooth their path in life is somehow cheating. In a professional setting, perhaps that's true (though I always maintain you catch more flies with honey than with vinegar). But giving your husband a saucy incentive to help you get jobs out of the way so you can *both* have some fun later is hardly a betrayal of the suffrage movement.

The stark truth is that if you deny a man sex for long enough, he *will* eventually seek it elsewhere.

> 'Women who feel secure in their marriages because their husbands love them think they don't have to bother with sex any more. They think he's kind of obliged to stay around no matter how badly you treat him.
>
> 'I don't understand why women don't get that sex is the main need men have. It's not just about getting laid, it's about closeness and tenderness, establishing a connection between the two of you. If she gives herself physically to me, I can give myself emotionally to her – and isn't that what women want?
>
> 'But when a woman won't sleep with you, the need for sex is all you can think about. You feel rejected and un-desirable and unvalued in so many ways. In the end, you've got no choice but to find a woman who will.'
>
> *Clive, 38, electrician*

Fringe benefits

Bitches understand about feminine wiles. They know what men need, and how to give it to them. So what kind of women are they, these hussies who slither like snakes into another woman's marital bed? And why don't they have a nice big red 'B' helpfully branded on their foreheads?

In a sense, some of them do.

You can divide mistresses into two camps. In one, we have the mercenary, who-needs-a-husband-when-you-can-borrow-somebody-else's, professional mistresses. These are the girls who chase expensive baubles and trinkets, meals at five-star restaurants and weekends in Paris on someone else's dime. Unless the man involved is *very* rich (and too stupid to get a pre-nup) they don't usually want him on a full-time basis, and would never *dream* of getting involved in any domestic duties 'such as sock washing, food shopping, or the boring duties that go with matrimony', as the inestimable Ms Symonds puts it. 'Let his wife have the pleasure of washing his dirty laundry after he's been having fun with you.'

These women are after the fringe benefits, a bit of fun (yes, adultery is *such* a hoot), and maybe a job or promotion. They're not hard to identify, and frankly, any man who fucks them and doesn't understand the nature of the business transaction is a dumb shit who deserves all he gets.

The tricky ones to spot are those in the other camp. These are the women who don't *seem* like Bitches. The ones who 'fall in love' and 'can't help it'. They can be anyone: you, me, your sister, your *mother*.

Mousy girls. Dull girls. Flashy, brazen extroverts. Wrinkled old battleaxes you'd think long past it. Sweet young teenagers you once *babysat* for.

Women you least suspect. Women you *trust*.

Closer than sisters

A woman I know, Kate, met her best friend, Jocelyn, at their sons' playgroup seventeen years ago. They'd both just moved to the Wirral, Kate from London and Jocelyn from Devon. Both had given up good jobs to follow their husbands, and were in their mid-thirties, lonely and a bit bored.

They swiftly struck up a firm friendship, cemented when they each became pregnant again within a month of each other.

Over the next ten years, they morphed into one extended family. Kate's husband, Colin, got on well with Jocelyn's long-term partner, Theo. They holidayed together in Spain every year, and took the kids skiing *en masse* during the winter half-term. When Kate's mother died suddenly, it was Jocelyn who looked after the children and helped her get through it. When Jocelyn's sister was diagnosed with breast cancer, Kate ferried her to and from the hospital if Jocelyn couldn't make it. The two women were so close that when Jocelyn found herself unexpectedly pregnant for a third time, and debating whether to keep the baby, Kate volunteered to have a third child to keep her company.

Six years ago, when the two sets of children were thirteen, ten and one, Kate booked the two families' holiday to Spain as usual. In fact, she was particularly looking forward to it, as Colin had been having a rough time at work and they hadn't been able to spend much time together.

For the first week or so, everything was fine. Kate and Jocelyn sat in the sunshine, drinking piña coladas and taking turns to supervise the children while the men went off snorkelling and sailing together. They gossiped about their husbands, their kids, mutual friends. There was no sign anything was amiss.

Then, four days before the end of the holiday, Jocelyn and Colin came over and sat next to Kate as she lounged by the pool.

'There's something we have to tell you,' Jocelyn began.

Calmly, she explained that Colin and she were having an

affair. They'd been sleeping together for more than eighteen months. In fact, Jocelyn's youngest child was *Colin's*, not Theo's. For a year and a half, Jocelyn had downed Chardonnay in Kate's kitchen, tucked into Kate's home-made lasagne, borrowed Kate's clothes and given no hint she was also borrowing Kate's husband.

'Theo was off jet-skiing on his own that morning,' Kate says now. 'Jocelyn said they hadn't wanted to ruin the holiday, but they just couldn't keep up the pretence any more. She told me I couldn't tell Theo until we got home. He might get violent, she said. She didn't want him upsetting the children.

'The awful thing was, I knew Theo, and I knew she was right. He *did* have a terrible temper. So for the next four days, I had to pretend nothing was wrong. Can you *imagine* how difficult that was?'

Worse was to come. When they returned to England and the news was finally broken to Theo, he moved out and took a high-paying new job in London – while Colin moved in with Jocelyn and her three children.

Kate had always been the breadwinner in the family, whilst Colin, a struggling writer, had looked after the children. Now, Kate was forced to hire an au pair for the youngest child (the child she'd had in part to please Jocelyn) and could no longer afford to pay the mortgage on their large detached house. With no child support from Colin, she was forced to sell up and move into a terraced house she hated. Meanwhile, Theo's new job meant he paid generous maintenance and child support to Jocelyn, whose life barely changed aside from the man in her bed. Naturally Kate's children loved staying in the big house with their father and their best friends, and would come home enthusing about how wonderful it all was. Even now, six years later, Kate can't tell me the story without crying.

Keep your friends close, and your (fr)enemies closer.

Bitches frequently turn out to be someone you know; sometimes even your best friend, or your sister. After all, who's better placed to undermine you than a woman who knows you inside and out?

For years you've told her secrets you haven't shared with your husband or boyfriend. She knows where every body in your relationship is buried. She knows your weaknesses – and his – and exactly how to undercut you and chip away at your relationship.

I'm not saying you can't leave your mother in the same room as your husband for five minutes in case she jumps him. Let's not get carried away. But realize that just because you're paranoid doesn't mean they're not out to get you.

Be alert. Be *aware*. Your relationship is *never* a done deal.

The better a husband he is to you, the more another woman is going to notice and decide she wants some of that. Don't make the mistake of resting on your laurels and assuming that your work is done. A little jealousy is a good thing. It'll stop you taking your man for granted.

You may be quite sure he loves you, and only you. You may well be right. But I'd keep reading, just in case.

In a nutshell

- It may not be fair, but men got the brawn, the penises and the small brains
- Girls, it's in our genes: we're all Bitches under the skin
- Leave it too late to find a man, and all the nice single ones will be gone
- There's only one word for women who get paid for bedroom favours . . . and it's not 'chambermaid'
- Breaking news: men like sex. (Who knew?)
- The only women you can trust are . . . um . . . let's come back to that one . . .

Chapter Three

Love Rat Stats*

Three out of four men will cheat on their wives and/or girlfriends
One in four men has more than four affairs
Fewer than one in ten men having an affair will leave their wife for their mistress
Three-quarters of men who do marry their mistress will later divorce her
80 per cent of men and women who divorce because of an affair ultimately regret their decision
The richer, more successful and better educated a man is, the more likely he is to have an affair – but the *less* likely he is to leave his wife
88 per cent of 'alpha males' cheat
85 per cent of women who suspect their lover is cheating are correct
50 per cent of women discover their partner's first affair (which means 50 per cent *don't* . . .)
Only 46 per cent of men believe online affairs are adultery
94 per cent of men don't think flirting is being unfaithful
Ten years after divorce, just 10 per cent of couples

(husbands and wives) have a better quality of life

Post-divorce, men are financially 25 per cent better off. Women are 20 per cent worse off

Given the chance, nearly 80 per cent of men would remarry their ex-wife

Almost 60 per cent of men having an affair are happy in their marriage

68 per cent of spouses find out about an affair when their partner confesses

In a quarter of cases, the spouse discovered the truth when they found evidence of the affair themselves

Only in 7 per cent of cases did someone else (including the mistress) tell them

Almost two-thirds of women regularly sneak a look at their partner's private text messages and emails, particularly when they suspect him of being unfaithful

When they snoop, more than one in five women find positive proof of infidelity

*See bibliography for sources.

Chapter Four
Snoop on the Dog

Men are stunningly predictable. They like blow-jobs. They like sport. They like beer. Unless given a list and forcibly directed not to deviate from it on pain of death, they buy their wives and girlfriends abysmal Christmas presents like bathroom scales, engine oil and oil filters, plastic flip-top rubbish bins and electric potato peelers. (Yes, these are real, honest-to-God examples from, now ex, boyfriends and husbands.)

They like their women to look and feel and behave like *women*. By which they generally mean pneumatic, old-fashioned girls who follow the Jerry Hall philosophy: be a maid in the living room, a cook in the kitchen and a whore in the bedroom.

A recent survey discovered that half of all men prefer women with long, wavy hair to all other styles and lengths combined. Well, who'd have thought it? Big boobs, short skirts, a nice smile . . . it's not rocket science.

It's this startling unoriginality that makes it so easy for Bitches to steal them; but it's also what makes it child's play for *us* to catch them when they stray.

I don't want to make you paranoid (oh, all right, I do . . . only because I care about you), but there is a reason you picked up this book. Apart from the *really* funky cover, of course.

If you've read this far, you should already be looking at every woman who crosses your path as a husband-stealing hussy.

The question you should now be asking yourself is: is my man already cheating? That's what the next few chapters will help you discover.

Is your man the cheatin' kind?

- **Did he sleep with a lot of women before you?**
- **Does he have more female than male friends?**
- **Do his friends screw around?**
- **Has he cheated on previous girlfriends?**
- **Did his father ever cheat on his mother?**
- **Does he think hookers/oral sex/virtual affairs don't count as cheating?**
- **Is he a thrill chaser?**

When a man has an affair, he usually follows a well-thumbed script. Hushed phone calls, late nights 'working', returning home reeking of cheap perfume and peddling cheaper lies. There's no reason for a woman to be the last to know. Unless she *wants* it that way.

Some women deliberately choose to turn a blind eye. If you know your husband is a philanderer and will (a) never be faithful but also (b) never actually *leave* you, and you've decided to accept it, then you may wish to delve no further. Knowing that he's cheating in general terms is a great deal easier to live with than knowing he bought twenty-two-year-old Lulu a Cartier bracelet when he took her to the Georges V Hotel in Paris over the last bank-holiday weekend.

If this is the case, skip the next few chapters and go straight to Chapter Twelve: Don't Get Mad, Get Diamonds, just in case you ever decide to skip town and get the hell out of Dodge.

However, you *can* still stop him cheating. If you're prepared to put the work in. But I must warn you, part of that will involve facing some very uncomfortable truths. If you're ready for that, keep reading.

A common fear is that if you find out he's cheating and confront him with his infidelity, it might propel him into his girlfriend's arms. Not if you handle it properly, it won't; we'll get to this in Chapter Nine: Beat the Bitch.

Remember: discovering he's having an affair doesn't automatically mean he has to know you know, and certainly not straight away. Knowledge – *your* knowledge – is power.

If the idea that your husband might be tempted to cheat were never to cross your mind, you wouldn't be exactly going out of your way to minister to your marriage. A woman who keeps an eye on her relationship is a woman who's not taking it for granted.

You need to take its temperature on a regular basis, and if it seems a bit under the weather now and again, apply some TLC. 'Don't ask, don't tell' is not a recipe for marital success. I can't tell you how many times in the course of my researching this book a woman wailed to me, 'But he never *said* he wasn't happy!'

He shouldn't have to. You should make it your business to know.

Make lemonade

Right about now, you may be thinking you wish you'd never opened this bloody book, because you don't think you really want to know after all.

But I promise you, if he *is* having an affair, not knowing about it is the worst situation to be in. In this instance, ignorance *isn't* bliss. Many men have a fling almost by mistake; the last thing they really want is a fully fledged affair. Heading it off at the pass doesn't necessarily mean making him 'fess up, although you may choose that route. But if you know about it, you can finally become proactive, instead of a victim. Surely that's a better place to start?

Just as importantly, most men signal their potential for infidelity *before* they actually do anything about it. Affairs usually develop over a period of time; even Accidental Adulterers (we'll get to this in Chapter Seven: Not All Affairs Are Equal), who never imagined they'd ever want to cheat but suddenly wake up one morning in bed with Shannon from Accounts, signal their readiness to stray well in advance, without even knowing it. If you pick up on these warning signs early, you've got a fighting chance of nipping the whole thing in the bud, saving yourself a heap of heartache and headaches.

Once you find out the facts, the ball – or, rather, *his*

balls – are in your court. If it turns out he's playing away, at least you can take control of the situation and make a cool, considered decision about how to handle things.

I know – trust me, *I do know* – how hard it is to be cool and considered if you find out your man is dipping his wick elsewhere. But you can have your nervous breakdown and nurse your broken heart later. First, you have to protect yourself.

Sometimes an affair can be a wake-up call for a relationship. No one's dumb enough to suggest it's a *good* thing, but if life gives you lemons, you can do worse than make lemonade. Finding out he's gone to someone else for what he used to get from *you* will force you (a) to decide if you want to salvage the relationship and (b) to say hi to the elephant in the room: the fact that however happy *you* think you are, something in your relationship clearly isn't working.

If you bury your head in the sand and refuse to acknowledge the truth, if only to yourself, he might take your apparent inattention as a sign he should be with the Bitch.

Should the worst happen and your marriage blows up in your face, at least you'll have had time to get your ducks in a row, so you don't suffer emotionally or financially any more than you have to. Trust me: *he'll* have prepared things long before he walks.

Your future's at stake. You could well need to find yourself a lawyer; you'll certainly want to keep a close eye on the family finances. You'd be shocked to discover how many supposedly 'decent' family men start to salt money away when they decide to leave their wives, and it has nothing to do with how much they earn. *It's my money*, they reason, *I've got every right to do with it what I want.*

All that love and romance, all those promises, for better for worse . . . in the end, when the relationship dies, it always comes down to money.

You may not like to think about it, but how *would* you cope if you woke up and found you suddenly had to manage all the bills alone? Food, mortgage, school fees, car insurance . . . don't just assume that he'll continue to provide for you and the kids if he ups and leaves. Let's face it, if he can walk out and abandon you after everything he promised, he could do anything.

Never be the kind of woman who leaves all the finances to a man. Even if your relationship is blissful, you should know what's hidden under which mattress. What would you do if your beloved (heaven forbid) was hit by a bus? Ask Whoopi Goldberg to hold a séance so you can ask him where he hid it?

So yes, for all the above reasons, and no matter how much it hurts, *you need to know if your man is having an affair.*

The smoking gun

One final topic we need to discuss before we get down and dirty. To snoop or not to snoop?

It's a tricky one, this. We all do it, they know we do it, but none of us wants to admit it.

A while back, my (current; second) husband was going out shopping. 'Will you be gone long?' I asked. 'I need to know if I've got time to go through your credit-card statements and see if I like what you've bought me for Christmas.'

He gawped at me, not quite sure if I was kidding or not.

'You keep them in that red file at the back of your wardrobe, right?' I added, straight-faced. 'I'll just have a quick look and then I'll be done. You'll never even know I was there.'

Recent research by security firm Symantec found that almost two-thirds of women regularly sneak a look at their partner's private text messages and emails, particularly when they suspect him of being unfaithful. A poll by the Lifetime cable network found that 67 per cent of women admitted to spying on their partners (and you can bet your life the *real* figure is much higher).

Detective agencies offering sophisticated 'honeytrap' stings have flourished in recent years, as women flex their new financial muscle and refuse to be the last to know.

'Psychologically, it's almost more painful to fret and worry about an unproven suspicion as opposed to getting actual proof. Women tend to expect that they'll meet a brick wall when they ask directly for some information. When we expect the worst – like an affair – we assume we won't get an honest answer.

'On the whole, it's hard to justify snooping as people should be able to have private lives. But if a woman knows a man is lying about something . . . only by doing a little bit of snooping will they get to the truth. If you love someone, but they blatantly lie to you, snooping is sometimes the only resort.'

Dr Pam Spurr, *Sensational Sex* (Robson Books)

If you check up on him, and he's innocent, well, no harm done, right?

But snooping carries a risk. As with eavesdropping, you often learn something you don't like. When we check up on our partners, more than one in five of us find a smoking gun.

Men don't tend to keep good news secret; the things they hide away are usually the things they don't want you to find.

There are several schools of thought on this one, and how far you go is very much a personal decision. Many of the signs of infidelity are subtle but obvious – yes, I know that sounds like a contradiction, but bear with me here. What I mean is that they're out in the open: they're changes in his behaviour or habits or appearance that you don't have to be Hercule Poirot to spot. If he drops ten pounds, buzz-cuts his hair, and puts a bolt on his home-office door, it's hardly an invasion of privacy for you to notice.

Other clues require a bit more . . . digging. Well, *prying*, really. The kind of poking around you want to shut the curtains for.

Then there's the whole-hog option: the private detective, the honeytrap, the DNA tests . . . Oh, yes, there's a whole host of goodies out there for the suspicious spouse, as Dr Luisa Dillner points out in her book *Love by Numbers*. CheckMate (www.getcheckmate.com), for example, will enable you to suss out that iffy stain on the picnic blanket that you know had nothing to do with you:

> . . . the revolutionary home use semen detection test kit that instantly detects traces of dried semen that can be found in underwear after sex. Sold around the world since 1999 CheckMate detects even the smallest trace

amounts of semen and can give you the instant information you need to deal with an impossible situation.

Then there's LoveDetect (www.lovedetect.com), a voice-
analysis service that promises to tell you if 'your sweetheart'
is 'really into you' just by talking with them on the phone:

> Personal ads, body language and shyness can all give
> wrong impressions – but the voice never lies. Voice
> patterns reflect the internal thought-process, or 'brain
> activity', as it takes place during general conversation
> or direct questioning. As our thoughts change our voice
> patterns change. LoveDetect measures and categorises
> these patterns.

The list goes on. Trust me, adultery is big business.

My own feeling? Know where to draw the line. If your
gut is telling you something isn't right, take the Bobbitt Quiz
in Chapter Six. (In fact, do it anyway. You never know.
Seriously.) If you don't have a slam-dunk case, but score in
the danger zone, I'd say you've got a moral search warrant
to snoop a little until you've either got confirmation or your
mind is put at rest. If that *really* means you have to swab his
underpants, do it; though I think if you're crawling around
the back seat of his car with a glass slide and a cotton bud,
you already know the answer.

In a good relationship, of course, both partners should be
able to have a degree of privacy. If you're already reading
his emails or checking his text messages, your relationship is
evidently missing a key ingredient: trust.

Which is *exactly* why you need to keep doing it.

You sad old pussy

As I've said, some signs are more obvious than others. We all know the clichés: phone hang-ups, lipstick on the collar, late nights at work. Or, as Ruth Houston would have it in her improbably named book *Is He Cheating on You? 829 Telltale Signs*, 'You walk in on him having sex with someone else. (Come home unexpectedly one day.) If you find this telltale sign, it's the only sign you need.' Don't you just love Americans?

But I digress. The first signs that most of us notice are a little more subtle than finding his head clamped between some strange woman's thighs on our 600-thread percale sheets. It's usually more of an intuitive reaction to some sort of change in his behaviour or manner, a gut instinct that something isn't quite right, even if you can't put your finger on it.

Sometimes a chance remark suddenly sets bells ringing in your head. Others, it's more of a cumulative, growing feeling of unease. What's actually happening is that your smart-arse subconscious is spotting signs and changes that you, you blissful, happy idiot, have failed to notice, and is elbowing you as hard and as sharply as it is able (given that it's a metaphor) in the ribs.

If your man is cheating, there are certain inescapable changes he's going to have to make in his habits and routines. He's got to talk to her, for a start – unless he happens to be sitting next to her at work, keeps every communication verbal and kills anyone who happens to overhear them – that means phone calls (especially to and from his mobile), text messages and emails. The advances in technology make it easier than ever to have an affair, but they also make it far more likely that he'll leave a trail of evidence a mile wide for you to find.

Unless he's unbelievably rich, which gives him *carte blanche* to smell like a hobo and look like a warthog and *still* pull, he'll have to spruce up his act to get a new woman in his bed. You, the sad old pussy, put up with his farts, stone-washed jeans and growing pot belly. She won't. He's got to *seduce* her, the way he once seduced you. So he'll make changes to his appearance.

Even if he's not a Rothschild, he's going to have to shell out if he wants her to put out. He may not be able to run to an Elsa Peretti heart necklace from Tiffany (the adulterer's gift of choice: every other Bitch I spoke to seemed to have been given one – I told you men are predictable), but he'll still have to pay for meals out, cabs home, maybe for hotel rooms and dirty weekends away. All of which means you can *follow the money*.

He'll be obsessed with this affair: both with conducting it and with not getting caught. He could become a total bastard at home, snarling at you and going off on one at the least opportunity. Or he might be Mr Sweetness and Light, guiltily overcompensating for his after-hours shenanigans.

Either way, there'll be periods where he just isn't with it; he'll be distant, preoccupied, less attentive to you and the kids, less involved in shared activities, less interested in the family, and less willing to talk to you or spend time with you one-on-one.

The key thing to look for is *change*. Only you know what's normal for your man. It's pretty much impossible for him to cheat without changing *some*thing about himself, his lifestyle or his routine. Stay tuned, and you'll catch the bastard almost before he's zipped up his pants.

You really don't need to look any further if . . .

1. You walk in on them having sex. (Yes, it is what you think)
2. His best friend, the one he's supposed to be away paintballing with, comes by to ask if he fancies going out tonight for a beer
3. You pick up the phone to make a call and overhear him telling a woman he can't wait to be her tampon
4. You call that strange number on your phone bill and he answers
5. You ring his mobile when he's away on business and a woman picks up. (On purpose. The Bitch has been just dying for this chance)
6. You find a lacy bra down the back of the sofa (and it's not yours or your teenage daughter's)
7. You discover a tissue-wrapped gift of lingerie in the back of his wardrobe – and it's nowhere near your size
8. You find out he's bought a flat in town you knew nothing about
9. The gym he says he's been attending three times a week burned down in a fire last year
10. You discover a paternity suit in the mail

There is a *chance*, of course (yes, OK, I'll allow it), that some changes have a completely innocent explanation. Maybe a Wunderkind has joined his company and he's shit-scared he'll get thrown out on his ear if he doesn't work all the hours God sends. Perhaps he's secretly decided to compete in the London Marathon to impress you, and that's why he's hitting the tarmac morning, noon and night. He might be worried about money (God knows, aren't we all?), or his mother coming to stay, or whether Britain's going to join the euro after all.

Then again, he could be sowing his oats elsewhere and laughing his bloody arse off at your gullibility.

The main reason the wife is the last to know is usually because *she wants to be*. Women rationalize the evidence away because they desperately don't want it to be true. You believe the crap he feeds you because you *need* to.

So, enough with the bullshit, girlfriend. Get your head out of the sand and take a deep lungful of that coffee aroma.

One final point: if you're going to check up on him, *don't tell him what you're doing.*

You'd think this'd be obvious, right? But you'd be surprised how many women are so outraged or upset when they find one sign, they run straight home to have it out with him. He is then able to offer up a plausible excuse, get you off his back, and make bloody sure you don't catch him out in anything else again.

You need to keep your guard up and not give the game away until you're good and ready. Timing is everything. Don't lose the advantage of surprise. You want to get enough evidence to either clear him or get him bang to rights. If you're tempted to drop a hint about what you've learned to prove you're not stupid enough to have the wool pulled over your eyes, restrain yourself with the thought of how much you're going to make the bastard squirm when the time is right.

In a nutshell

- Men are predictable; when they deviate from their routines, it's for a reason
- Knowing he's cheating will give you time to arm and prepare yourself
- Never be the kind of woman who allows herself to be left high and dry financially
- Even if you don't want to snoop, be aware. Be observant
- The key to look for: change
- Don't lose the advantage of surprise and let him know you're on to him

Chapter Five

How Do I Cheat on Thee?
Let Me Count the Ways

Have I got you well and truly paranoid now? Good. Let's cut to the chase. We'll start where he does: in the bedroom.

It isn't always easy to pick up the changes here, because the cobwebs may have been gathering for quite a while – hence the arrival of the Bitch.

So, think hard, girls. How often have you had sex over the past year? (Over 365 and you can put this book down. The poor bugger's not cheating on you; he's *exhausted*.)

Now, how frequently are you having sex these days?

For once, it's not the number of shags a month that matters, but whether there's been a significant change – up *or* down.

Men often stop bonking their wives when they're getting it elsewhere because (a) *duh!* they're getting it elsewhere and (b) they feel a bizarre sense of loyalty to the Bitch, especially if they fancy themselves 'in lurve'.

Has he stopped feeling you up when you get out of the

shower? Does he come to bed late (especially after spending hours on the computer) so you're already asleep when he finally crawls under the covers? Does he plagiarize *your* pet excuses to avoid sex: I have a headache, I'm tired, I've got my period – OK, well maybe not that one. But you get the idea.

If and when you *do* have sex, it might be perfunctory (if *that's* nothing new, maybe you should let the Bitch keep him. Some men have yet to figure out that being a sexual athlete does *not* mean coming first).

He might not meet your eyes when you're At It. And remember the kissing thing in *Pretty Woman*? No mouth-to-mouth for Cinderella tart Julia Roberts because it's 'too personal'? So, does he still kiss you when he comes home from work? Before you go to sleep? And – crucially – when you have sex?

Or perhaps he can't get it up at all. This is one of the most common signs the bastard's having an affair; and it *isn't* that common, it *doesn't* happen to every guy, and it *is* a big deal.

Yes, it might be tiredness. It might be the recession. (Although history shows that whenever there's a war on, birth rates go up, so clearly the stress of imminent death or mutilation doesn't put a crimp in most men's stride. Funny how your man is such a delicate little flower he wilts at the first whisper of the words 'deflation' and 'negative equity', isn't it?) Sadly, it's far more likely that he shot his wad with her a couple of hours ago, and hasn't recharged the batteries yet. Or – less likely – maybe at least *one* part of him (yeah, the bit that makes all the decisions) feels a little bit guilty.

If he can't get it up twice or more in a row, you should be on red alert. If it's not his prostate, he's probably getting prostrate, and not with you.

Oh, and the icing on the cake? He'll likely say it's *your* fault.

'Tom and I were on a romantic break to Hawaii – my mother was looking after the baby, and we had an entire fortnight to ourselves. It should have been perfect: plenty of sunshine, crystal-clear aquamarine seas, nothing to do all day but relax and spend time together. Everything was fine to begin with, but when we tried to make love, Tom couldn't get an erection. At first, he blamed it on the wine and the long journey, but it kept on happening. I told him it didn't matter, but he screamed at me that of course it did, and if I'd got my figure back after the baby, maybe he'd be able to fancy me. I was so hurt; I'd worked really hard to get back into shape, and actually weighed less than before I got pregnant!

'Things weren't any better when we got home. Eventually, we stopped trying. Three months after our holiday, I found out he'd been having an affair for over a year. And he had the cheek to blame it on me!'

Lesley, 31, triage nurse

Sometimes cheating husbands want sex *more* often than usual, because it's on their minds all the time – the thought of the Bitch in that sexy lace thong he just bought her from La Perla/Selfridges/M&S (delete as income-appropriate) makes him horny, but thanks to your tiresome existence she's not always accessible when he wants it, and as we all know, any hole will do in a pinch.

He's also flicked through enough women's mags standing at the checkout in Tesco to know that *not* shagging your wife is a big giveaway when you're screwing around, so he'll bend over backwards (sometimes literally) to make sure you get yours often enough to keep you nice and trusting.

But it's very hard to lie *thoroughly* when you're having sex. It's a bit like driving a car: there are so many little things to remember, it's hard to keep track of them all, so your brain kicks into auto-pilot and does things for you.

Which means that, if you take the time to notice, he'll give himself away. He'll tease your nipples with the pad of his thumb, for example, instead of twisting away at them like they're volume controls. He might try out new positions, new tricks, new places (the kitchen table, for example; dreadfully unhygienic, I always think). Either he's learning these shenanigans *from* her, or practising on you *for* her. (Say after me: an Infidel has no shame.)

Perhaps he's been begging you for years to try a bit of rear entry, to the point where you were tempted to buy a cucumber and stick it up his arse to see how he liked it. But now you think about it, he hasn't mentioned it once in the past few months . . .

Well, come on, woman! When has a man ever stopped banging on about something he really wants in bed unless he's started *getting it elsewhere*?

Another little pointer that there's a worm in your apple: birth control.

Is he suddenly *very* helpful about reminding you to take your pill every morning? Or has he started wearing condoms, 'just to be on the safe side'?

If you find condoms or condom wrappers anywhere, and the two of you don't use them, don't kid yourself: *there isn't an innocent explanation.* They're *not* left over from his student days, they're *not* his brother's, and Boots *isn't* handing them out free because it's Condom Awareness Day.

Some signs are so bloody obvious they don't require explanation. In addition to actually catching him in flagrante, into this category come STDs (assuming you're not misbehavin' too), a phone call from his girlfriend (no smoke without fire: *why* would the 'bunny boiler' from his office want to 'set him up' if he hadn't given her good reason?), lipstick on his boxers, semen on the car seats, or a woman on your doorstep cradling a baby.

If it looks like a fuck, sounds like a fuck, walks like a fuck . . .

Forever in blue jeans

A man having an affair – or even thinking about it – wants to make himself hotter and sexier for the Bitch in his sights. Which means getting himself, and his wardrobe, back into shape.

For years, while *you've* been working your arse off (literally) at the gym, highlighting and conditioning your hair, moisturizing your face, plucking your eyebrows, tinting your eyelashes, flossing your teeth, Botoxing your wrinkles, filling your laughter lines, exfoliating your skin, massaging your cellulite, waxing your bikini line, shaving your legs, pumicing your feet and clenching your Kegels, he's been happily cultivating love-handles, a paunch and a bald patch.

For you, the sad old pussy, he'll pick his feet, belch, inspect the contents of his nose and neck enough beers in front of the TV to turn into a pasty-faced dirigible.

For his new pussy, he'll stop at nothing to get in shape.

You'll notice the change in his wardrobe first. If he's meeting her at or through work, he'll suddenly spruce up his office clothes: buy a few new shirts, some fancy silk ties. He might start to wear cufflinks or ditch the 'fun' socks the kids buy him every Christmas.

He'll mumble something about 'dressing for the job you want, not the one you have' and whip out the 'emergency' Amex to splurge on a Brioni suit (whilst bitching at you for taking advantage of the Boden summer sale).

That tatty old briefcase he's toted around for years? Gone, traded in for something leather and shiny and 'executive'.

Outside work, he might start dressing down or 'young', ditching the stuffy suits for casual cargos and fine cotton sweaters. Or he'll take his spending up a notch: the cheap trainers you thought he'd be buried in are elbowed out by stylish Pumas, the sweatshirts ditched for cashmere jumpers.

He'll get all gussied up for his regular sessions down the pub 'with the guys', or to nip out to get that oh-so-crucial part for the lawnmower. (The fact that he keeps on running vital errands for appliance parts but nothing ever gets fixed tells its own story.)

Changes in his preferred type of underwear are a dead giveaway. If your hygiene-averse, turn-them-inside-out-and-they'll-do-two-days Y-fronts slob is suddenly splashing out on jersey shorts or silk boxers and changing them twice a day, trust me, it has nothing to do with worrying about the correct temperature he should keep his testicles at.

If he's always been a bit of a peacock when it comes to clothes, and buying new ones is nothing unusual, look for changes in *style*.

Are the new suits a little sharper-cut, a bit younger and
. . . well, *flashier*? If he's a man who hasn't worn jeans since
Michael J. Fox was jumping Back to the Future, and suddenly he's sporting the latest low-rise left-weave denims
from a must-have label even *you've* barely heard of, he's not
doing it to please his mother.

Men are creatures of habit, remember. Once they've
found the brands, colours and styles they like, which usually
happens somewhere around the age of twenty-five, they
tend to settle into them for the duration.

As soon as they're in a long-term relationship, they generally stop even buying their own clothes. Basically, they'll
go from wearing whatever their mothers bought for them to
wearing whatever you pick out.

Hello? In other words, they wear what the women in
their life want them to wear.

If he's having an affair, he'll suddenly stop wanting you to
shop for him and start buying his own clothes. Once you've
come round from the shock, you should raise your Bitch
Alert status to High. There's only one reason he wants to
choose his own stuff: in his head, he's reverted to the single
life and wants to groom himself for the Bitch.

He might suddenly develop an interest in fashion; you'll
catch him with a copy of *GQ* – and no, it's *not* for the arti-
cles.

Check to see if any of his favourite items are missing from
his wardrobe. If so, he may be keeping them at the office to
change into after work when he meets her, or even leaving
them at her place. (If he leaves home in a pale blue shirt and
comes back in a green one, you didn't imagine it: he forgot
to change back.)

He may start to put on the odd load of laundry now and then 'to help you out'; don't faint with delight, he's just trying to get rid of tell-tale lipstick stains and the smell of her perfume before you notice.

He'll stop dumping his clothes over the back of the chair for you to pick up, and hang them up himself – yes, you're getting it: he's not being helpful, he just doesn't want you going through his pockets. (Make sure you do it anyway, of course. Once a week, whether he needs it or not.)

The image revamp isn't limited to his wardrobe. It *starts* there, because that's the easiest thing to alter, but you'll notice other subtle, and not-so-subtle, changes.

He might start to use Regaine on his bald patch, or colour his grey hair. If it's long, he might cut it; if he's sported the same short-back-and-sides since you met, he'll suddenly want to grow it. If he's got a moustache or beard, he might shave it off; if he's always been clean-shaven, he could suddenly sprout a fetching little boy-band goatee.

A keen adulterer will take forever in the bathroom, and when he comes out he'll smell of *your* bloody moisturizer. He'll shower far more than he ever used to, especially when he comes home: he's not washing off the 'city grime', he's washing off *her*.

He'll start wearing aftershave instead of going *au naturel*, or switch from the brand he's used since the day his voice broke. He'll suddenly decide his teeth need whitening, or get contact lenses instead of glasses. His breath will always smell minty fresh (you'll start to find breath fresheners *every*where).

And then of course there's his body. When a man who thinks changing channels with the TV remote is a workout suddenly joins a gym, a Bitch may well be at the bottom of it. He might buy one of those home gyms that clog up eBay every January and cost the same amount as a small car.

Or he could start jogging or playing tennis, both to get fit and as an excuse to go out and meet the Bitch. Every night, he'll be on the bedroom carpet doing push-ups. He'll go on a diet, or suddenly start banging on about the 'nutritional content' of his favourite shepherd's pie.

A sudden passion for sushi? A new-found interest in vegetarianism? *Cherchez la Bitch.*

Oh yes. One final note on his appearance, and this one comes straight from the Department of the Blindingly Obvious: *he'll stop wearing his wedding ring.*

A hard day's night

Means, motive and opportunity

As Sherlock would say, these are the three key factors when it comes to solving a crime; and that includes screwing around. Motive is easy: he's a man (see previous chapters). Means: he has a penis, hasn't he? Which leaves opportunity: easily provided by legitimately spending at least five full days out of seven – and a good many late nights, if he's a mind – far away from your suspicious, all-seeing eyes.

Overtime. Meetings. Business trips. Conferences. Courses. Paintball bonding sessions. There's no end to the excuses he can come up with. It's like letting a kid loose in a sweetshop.

Yes, we all know there's a recession on, and we've all got to work twice as hard for twice as long to hang on to our jobs. Call me cynical, but if your nine-to-five clock watcher is suddenly crawling in the door just in time to catch the end credits of the *Ten o'Clock News*, I don't think he's developed a new-found commitment to widgets.

He thinks he's safe, because it's hard to keep tabs on a man at work; and of course some of his favourite excuses will, occasionally, be true.

You don't have to be shacked up with Watson, however, to catch him out.

Have you ever called the office to speak to him, only to find he's taken a day off you didn't know about? Does he tell you he's working late, but no one answers the phone when you call to tell him his dinner's in the dog? (No, the switchboard girl *didn't* go home early. Have I taught you *nothing*?)

A sudden increase in business trips, without a concomitant promotion or change in job, is a classic giveaway. It's pretty much the only regular excuse he can use to spend a full night away from you.

Ditto an abrupt surge in the amount of time he has to spend 'entertaining' (I bet he is) important clients after work.

Is he a bit hyper – *excited*, almost – before a business trip? Has he stopped asking you to come along the way he used to? Does the annual sales conference now take five days instead of three? If so, he's probably taking her, using a legitimate excuse to cover his illegitimate activities . . . Machiavelli was a pussy compared to a man trying to get his leg over.

If he doesn't want you to 'trouble yourself' dropping him off at the airport, he might be flying somewhere other than where he told you, or not even getting on a plane at all. Likewise his new willingness to unpack his own suitcase. He hardly wants you finding grass stains on his jeans when he was supposed to be at a sales pitch in New York.

Does he tell you he's going clay-pigeon -shooting or fishing with the guys, but when he comes home his equipment is as neat and shiny as it was the morning he left? (His shooting and fishing equipment, that is.)

He may generously encourage you to go off on trips with the girls – a spa weekend, a ski holiday – partly to get you out of the way so he can see the Bitch, and partly because he'll feel less guilty if he can tell himself (and her) that you 'practically lead separate lives'.

When he travels, instead of giving you a hotel phone number, he'll tell you to use his mobile because 'it's easier'. Well, yes: easier for him than having you know precisely where he is, of course.

Is he remarkably diligent about calling you morning and evening when he's away? Don't congratulate yourself just yet: he's doing it so you have no need to ring him and interrupt his 'meeting' with the Bitch.

Does he have to work on weekends and bank holidays? Does he leave for work much earlier than he used to (he's meeting the Bitch *en route* for a quickie, or changing his journey to work so he can travel part of it with her – all together now: *awwwww*)? Does he get a phone call at home on a Saturday afternoon and suddenly have to rush into the office to deal with an emergency?

Have you ever bumped into one of his colleagues' wives at Sainsbury's, and had her exclaim what a *shame* it is that you missed the office get-together last weekend, and is your mother feeling better now?

He'll tell you WAGs aren't invited to company parties any

more, or give you five minutes' notice so it's too late to get a babysitter, and generally do his best to discourage you from having any contact with his office. Well, *of course* he doesn't want you talking to anyone he works with! They might make mincemeat of his alibis and give the game away.

Keep your eyes open when you do connect with his colleagues: the Bitch could well be someone he works with. The running-off-with-his-secretary cliché is a cliché precisely because it's so often true. Men are lazy bastards, remember. Hence their tendency to shag nannies, secretaries and your sister. Why go searching for available totty when it's handily right there under your nose?

What happens when you drop by his office unexpectedly? Have the photos on his desk of the two of you in Greece last summer suddenly vanished? Where are the cute birthday cards the kids painted for him?

Does everyone seem a bit . . . well, *weird* around you? Nervous, almost?

Watch out for a particular woman acting a little too familiarly towards him, possessively bustling in with memos when you're trying to talk to him, or interrupting him with 'urgent' messages. She's staking her claim and marking out her territory. If she's not actually the Bitch, she knows damn well who is, and is *loving* having one up on you.

Follow the money

You should *always* know what your man is earning, regardless of whether you think he might be cheating on you or not. Don't be a pathetic little woman who can't get her pretty head around numbers. Take some responsibility here, and you'll be able to spot an affair pretty much the day he buys her the first vodka tonic.

Affairs cost money. He'll have to take her out, buy her gifts, stay at hotels. Later, as the affair gathers speed, he'll want to feather his love-nest and salt money away for a divorce he thinks you know nothing about.

So, is all that oft-referenced 'overtime' evidenced in his salary? Or does he work 24/7, and yet somehow you're still broke? Has he switched his salary deposit from your joint current account to a 'higher-interest account' he's set up in his name, and from which he's started paying the bills himself, so that you can't see how much he's earning?

He may think he's being clever, but the great thing about money is that unless you're an Al Qaeda money launderer, its movements leave a trail a mile wide.

The first thing you'll notice is that things may seem a bit tight financially. Once you've factored out your own inability to resist the aforementioned Boden catalogue, funds are still a bit lower than you can account for.

Are there frequent unexplained cash withdrawals from your joint account? Or regular payments from it that you know nothing about? These could be anything from secret credit cards to the rent on a shag-pad in town.

At the start of an affair, a man will try to pare down expenses at home so that he can meet his additional costs from your joint income without arousing your suspicion. Bills he's personally responsible for may be paid late as a result.

He might cancel insurance or other low-key monthly expenditure, such as the extra sports channels on cable, without telling you. He'll demand that you cut back on household expenses ('Don't you know there's a recession on, woman?') but won't attempt to pay off your joint debts or save money for a rainy day.

Astonishingly, he may even stop questioning you about how much *you're* spending on clothes, pedicures and magic anti-wrinkle creams. Men *never* do this unless (a) you're the sugar-mummy keeping them or (b) they've got a guilty conscience and don't want you to start quizzing them in return.

If you're not earning, he may now make it an issue where it never was one before, and insist that you find a job. He's got a dual motive here: in addition to bringing in some much-needed cash, he's laying the foundation for a divorce petition that will show you are capable of paying your own way, and will thus reduce your claim to maintenance from him.

If he's really dumb, he might actually charge the flowers and romantic dinners to his usual credit card, thinking that if you spot it he can explain it away as a present for his mother or a normal business expense. Once again, when you're casting your eyes over the credit-card bill, the key word is *change*: you're looking for expenses outside his normal pattern.

Many men having a long-term affair simply take out another card you know nothing about, and have the bills sent to their offices.

If you really want to play Sherlock, check out his credit score with a good credit-check agency. They usually provide a list of credit-card debts, so you'll be able to spot if there's an extra one in his name that you didn't know about.

However, this secret card will still need paying off somehow. If he doesn't service it from your joint account, he must have set up another bank account in his own name. Which means he's got to be diverting funds to it from his salary somewhere down the line.

Do the maths. You know (or you damn well should) what he earns. So is any money missing?

If you have savings or stocks that are worth anything, he may liquidate some of them to finance his affair. He could start shifting savings around, including the kids' school-fees fund, or suggest you put the house in his name 'for tax purposes'. He might want to pay off his parents' mortgage: a sneaky way of getting money out of the marital pot so you can't claim any of it in a divorce.

If you find paperwork for any of the above that you didn't know about – credit cards, bank and savings accounts, property or stock purchases and sales – *there isn't an innocent explanation.*

Can you hear me now?

Ah, the telephone. One of the great unsung sex aids, right up there with Cadbury's Flakes and pale turquoise Tiffany jewellery boxes.

It's simple: if he's having an affair, he's phoning her. And texting her. And emailing her. Even if he's sitting right next to her in the office.

It's what lovers *do*, even if they vow to be 'careful'. He might tell her not to call him at home, but she will, especially when the affair gathers pace. A flurry of wrong numbers and hang-ups *may* be teenagers getting their kicks (I'm feeling in a generous mood), but check your caller ID (if you don't have it, *get it*) or dial 1471. Teenage morons don't go to the trouble of hiding their number every time. Bitches do.

Even if she doesn't call, many men are reckless and/or stupid enough to call her from home; keep an eye on your home phone bill for an unknown number that keeps coming up. More commonly, he'll use his mobile, especially if it's a work phone and the bills don't get sent home. Trouble is, he knows these handy little devices can also prove a smoking gun, so if he starts to keep his mobile phone glued to his hip, *wonder why*.

Ditto if he moves the charger out of the kitchen to somewhere you're less likely to access his phone when he plugs it in, such as his study. If you do check it, and you'd be a fool not to, be very, *very* suspicious if he's deleted his call history. Why would an innocent man bother?

Check out his address book. He might not be quite daft enough to list the Bitch under her real name, but be wary of male Christian names that lack a surname, and are not those of close friends you know. Betcha 'Joe', 'Mike' and 'Frank' are really 'Joanna', 'Michelle' and 'Francesca'.

A man in the throes of an affair will be generally *weird* around the phone. Jumping on it the second it rings. Using his mobile when it'd be easier and cheaper to pick up the home phone. Whispering or mumbling into it. Developing whiplash by double-checking you're not in earshot while he's talking. Taking calls through into another room (*business*? At three o'clock on a Sunday afternoon?).

He may put his mobile on vibrate when he's home, so you don't know when he's getting calls and texts. It *always* seems to be on; except when you're trying to reach him, of course.

He's not in a bad area. There is reception. His battery isn't dead. Trust me.

If he can't escape you when his mobile rings – such as when you're in the car together – he'll be nervous and edgy, either not taking the call at all, or talking in monosyllables and ending the conversation as soon as he can. When you ask him who it is, he'll be vague or irritable in his reply.

He always seems to be hanging up the phone when you walk into the room. He makes or receives calls at odd times of day: before breakfast, or after you've gone to bed. There never seem to be any messages left on the answer machine any more (because he's listening to them first, just to be on the safe side).

You leave the house, but have to go back for something you forgot, and he's on the phone. A week later, it happens again.

When he calls you to tell you he's got to 'work late', there are suspicious noises in the background (music, the clink of restaurant china) or none at all (he's at her place). He talks in a strained whisper as if he doesn't want to be overheard, and when you tell him you love him, he pretends he didn't catch it, or mutters a terse 'You too' back.

Some clues are more obvious than Gerard Depardieu's nose on your face. If you find a mobile phone you didn't know existed, for instance. A husky female 'Hello' when you press Redial or dial 1471.

Or when you overhear him whispering sweet, lust-filled nothings – my personal *modus discoverus* and, I imagine, second in pain only to walking in on the two of them in bed.

Come up and play with my hard drive

While we're on the subject of technology . . .

Wireless connectivity. Bluetooth. Laptops, BlackBerries, tweeting, iPhones . . . so many ways for lovers to communicate; so many ways for dumb bastard husbands to get caught.

As with his mobile, he won't be able to resist hooking up with the Bitch online. He may confine much of it to his office hours (really, it's a miracle the man finds time to write his name at the top of the page, never mind put in a full day's work) but you can bet your pentium chip his little fingers will be busy texting or typing at home whenever he thinks your back's turned.

Late-night sessions in front of the computer screen, early-morning dashes to check his emails, closing his laptop the minute you walk in the room, overly familiar IMs (instant messages) popping up on screen – do I have to spell it out?

Does he delete files and histories to cover his online tracks? Set up a separate email account 'because he's fed-up with all the spam'? Change his password on a weekly basis?

If he's screwing around, there will be incriminating emails. Human nature is the same the world over. Lovers invariably feel the need to bombard each other with the most sentimental, embarrassing drivel (just check out the classifieds on 14 February). He may delete them, but it won't take much to exhume them; if you don't know how to minister the virtual kiss of life, just talk to one of those pimply children at a computer superstore, or download some software from a site like www.recover-my-email.com or www.paraben.com.

Men often forget to empty their computer's recycle bin. When he's talking to the Bitch, the only hard drive he's thinking about is the one between his legs. No matter how clever he thinks he is, he'll leave a virtual trail. All you have to do is follow it.

If you can't *ever* get a single moment alone to play with his laptop, ask yourself *why*. An innocent man doesn't keep his computer under lock and key.

Love me, love my penis

He has one other sex toy you need to think about, and it's often overlooked. His car.

Think of it as an extension of his dick; after all, he does. Are there strange smells, such as her perfume, or cigarettes when he doesn't smoke? Stains (yes, I know, yuk, but fucking is a messy business)? Strands of hair that don't match yours, or the dog's – one excuse from an Infidel whose wife I interviewed. And oddly accurate, when you think about it.

A single earring on the floor, condoms in the glove compartment, wads of used tissues shoved beneath the seat?

If your man is forty and the inside of his car resembles that of a hormonal seventeen-year-old, that's probably because he's screwing one in it.

Has he started to keep a picnic blanket in the boot, 'in case the car breaks down'? A change of clothes 'for the gym' (check to see if his holdall really contains workout gear)? Are there more of those bloody breath-mints in the loose-change tray?

Don't even get me started on the lacy black bra hidden

beneath the front seat. If you find one (a) he's having an affair; and (b) she planted it there.

You don't lose your bra or knickers in a car by mistake.

Sorry. Back here in the real world, it doesn't happen. What *does* happen is that she decides to up the ante by leaving her bra for you to find, and thereby forcing a showdown. This comes under the same general heading as phone calls from the Bitch telling you she's sleeping with your husband, and other ways she may try to force the pace. Don't give her the upper hand. Keep your cool, and stay in the driving seat. (Give me a break, I think I'm allowed the odd pun.)

Less obvious indicators are those that simply signal he has a regular passenger in the car who isn't you. If you have to adjust the position of the passenger seat or the AC vents more than once or twice, or the radio is tuned to a channel he *never* listens to, or there are CDs of music he wouldn't usually buy, you have good reason to be suspicious.

Greeks bearing gifts

People give presents for all sorts of reasons: *I want to go to bed with you. I'm sorry I fucked up. Get off my back and leave me alone. Please don't tell my wife. I'm screwing the babysitter and I feel really bad about it. Just take the diamonds and close your eyes.*

If he starts sporting things he'd never buy himself – funky ties, cufflinks, a watch – then *some*one bought them for him. Likewise trinkets that may pop up around the house: executive toys, a shell photo-frame, silly knick-knacks (mementoes of their secret trysts, no doubt).

Beware if your usually conscientious but uninspired husband either suddenly starts giving you really crap gifts like a fax machine or toilet brush (yes, more real-life examples) or over-compensates and splashes out on a £6,000 Cartier love bangle. That's just the guilt talking.

If he suddenly starts remembering Valentine's Day when he always forgot it before, it's probably because she's reminding him.

Likewise if the calibre of your Christmas gifts unexpectedly goes up. He's getting his good taste from someone.

He may stop buying you presents altogether, because he can't afford it and doesn't really care; or he may shove a cheque in your hand and tell you to 'buy yourself something pretty'. My ex-husband did that once. I bought diamonds. *Big* ones. Strangely, he didn't do it again.

I shouldn't have to tell you by now what it means if you find gifts, or receipts for gifts, that you never receive (like poor Emma Thompson in *Love, Actually*. Every time I watch that movie, my heart bleeds for her). A sneaky cheat favourite: he buys a big bottle of your favourite perfume, but it never shows up in your stocking. *He's given it to her so that you both smell the same.*

Home cheat home

Once you start looking, you'd be amazed how much incriminating evidence you may find, especially if he's stupid enough, and ruthless enough, to bring her home when you're away.

I once dated a man I assumed was single, since he told me that was the case and I had no reason to suppose otherwise. I stayed over at his flat at least twice a week for nearly three months. The relationship petered out and we split up, at which point he confessed he had been living with another woman the entire time! She was often away on business, which was presumably when he had me come over. He must have spent his life tidying. I never saw a single sign anywhere in that flat that there was a woman living there. Not a tampon or a cushion or a chick-flick DVD. On the contrary, I often left a change of clothes there, or my hairdryer. Presumably he hid it all the second the door shut behind me, and got out all her stuff again. Can you *imagine* how much energy that must have taken?

Be wary if the guest ashtray has been recently washed, though you don't recall having had visitors. Take note of unfamiliar shampoo in the shower, or the regular appearance of a type or brand of alcohol neither of you drink. Once could be an unexpected visitor; twice and he's guilty as sin.

Has he changed the sheets while you were away at your sister's? (Frankly, I think this is as cut-and-dried as walking in on them going at it. Come on: *a man change the sheets unasked*?)

Is there a new key on his keyring (to her flat)? Stubs for movies you didn't go to? Dog or cat hairs on his suit, when you don't have either? Cryptic notes – often just initials – in his desk diary?

If you don't notice obvious things like these, then you deserve to lose him, because you're not noticing *him*.

Stow the attitude

Remember how we talked about intuition? Well, all right, *I* did. You didn't get a word in, but bear with me here, I'm just trying to be inclusive.

Intuition is when your clever old subconscious spots things your oblivious conscious mind glosses over. The warning messages get passed down the line, and eventually pitch up in your brain as a 'feeling' or 'hunch'. *Trust them.* The stats don't lie: 85 per cent of women who suspect their lover is cheating are correct.

It's less obvious, but the way your man acts towards you can tell you as much as finding the Bitch's knickers under your bed.

OK, maybe not *quite* as much. You won't know she's got a big arse from his attitude, the way you would from finding her outsize underwear. But hey, let's just assume she's got a huge bum anyway.

An affair affects the way he thinks and feels about you. He might despise you for not knowing. He could feel guilty. He may simply stop giving a damn about you at all.

Marvellous, isn't it, how a man in the wrong will get angry with you, as if it's *your* fault. But then, in his mind, *it is*. If he can find a way to blame you for his affair, he can justify to himself what he's doing.

He might become unusually irritable and impatient with you. The fact that you still appear to be breathing will drive him up the wall. He'll bitch all the time, criticizing your clothes, your accent, your cooking.

'The bank I worked for had posted us to Kuala Lumpur for three years, and at James's suggestion I invited my parents to come out for our first Christmas (his own had died years before). They booked their flights, and everything was arranged. Then suddenly, James started acting strangely. He criticized everything I did and snapped at me over little things for no reason. Things came to a head when we went out for dinner on my birthday, a few weeks before Christmas. He started saying all these really spiteful things, like how my parents were sponges and leeches, and he was fed up having to "carry" them. It was all so unfair! By the time we got to dessert, I was in floods of tears. Even our waitress looked sorry for me.

'When I told my parents, they nearly cancelled their trip, but I persuaded them not to. I'm so glad I did: on New Year's Eve, I overheard James talking to his mistress on the phone, and discovered he'd been having an affair for more than four months behind my back.'

Rhianna, 36, investment analyst

He doesn't want to hear what you have to say, cutting you off when you try to talk to him; he'll never ask about your day.

He may give you the silent treatment, snap at you, or change the subject when you try to discuss your job, your friends, your family. Talking to him is like pulling teeth. You'll end up feeling like you're banging your head against a brick wall.

If he does deign to talk to you, he'll be a bloody smart alec, putting you down and sneering at your opinions. When you ask him what's wrong, he'll refuse to discuss it, or pretend he doesn't know what you mean. He'll belittle you in front of other people, or exclude you from the conversation.

He doesn't want to spend time with you any more, refusing to go antiquing or rock-climbing or whatever it was you once used to do together. (Beware. Not taking time to have fun together is one of the triggers for an affair.) When you come into a room, he leaves it. If you try to hold his hand, he pulls it away. He turns his head when you go to kiss him, so you get a mouthful of hair. He stops calling you by that hideously embarrassing but nonetheless loving pet name. He won't come with you to your parents' silver wedding anniversary party.

He's stubborn, uncooperative, preoccupied. He makes a huge song and dance if you ask him to do anything for you, or around the house. (Not to be confused with the benign, if infuriating, male auto response to anything that might remotely be deemed 'nagging'.)

You turn round one day in the kitchen to see him staring at you with a look of complete disdain. He'll wipe it off his face, but the blank, dead expression that's left behind isn't much of an improvement.

He'll pick fights with you over stupid things, which also gives him the excuse to storm out of the house and see the Bitch.

He'll keep suggesting you invite friends and family over; not because he's feeling nice and sociable, but because he doesn't want to spend a second alone with you that he doesn't have to. He'll encourage you to take up a hobby (evening classes, volunteer work, underwater basket-weaving) to free up large blocks of time for him to sneak off and do his own thing.

He doesn't seem to care what you do or where you go;

but at the same time, he takes an inordinate interest in the logistical minutiae of your day, so that he can work out when it's safe to see her.

He might start accusing *you* of cheating on *him*, to put you on the back foot and turn the spotlight away from him. He'll charge you with not trusting him, checking up on him, imagining things. Infidels always like to think you're a bit unstable. Again with the justification.

When you do something nice for him, he'll be overwhelmed with guilt, and he won't like that, so he'll be terse and ungrateful.

On the other hand, he might suddenly shower you with presents and flowers: guilt again. Don't throw them away out of hurt or pride. There's a great market in guilt gifts on eBay, so trade up.

If he suddenly becomes very attentive and unusually considerate towards you (this usually happens at the start of an affair; later on he's just the opposite), he's (a) trying to keep you sweet so you don't get suspicious, (b) swamped with remorse, or (c) just been dumped by the Bitch and is trying to get back in with you instead. Any hole in a pinch, remember.

Stepford husband

It's not just about the way he treats *you*. Does he generally seem to have undergone a personality transplant in recent months? Is your comfortable, reliably miserable old fart suddenly bouncing around like Tigger on speed? Is he suddenly quiet and withdrawn when he used to be open and outgoing? Or happy and good-tempered when he used to make Eeyore look cheerful? (OK, enough with the Pooh metaphors. I need to get out more.)

He might be much easier to get along with (he's getting what he needs elsewhere). He suddenly seems more confident (he's getting affirmation in the sack). He's got bags of energy, and you catch him smiling at nothing . . . remember that 'in lurve' feeling, ladies?

He could go the other way and turn into an (even more) cantankerous old grouch. Everything gets on his tits, he's in a permanently foul mood, he overreacts to the slightest thing. He's aggressive and belligerent, constantly picking fights with you, and he's even impatient with the kids.

'Andrew and I always seemed to be arguing, which hadn't been the pattern of our relationship at all. He suddenly started complaining about how I looked – my weight, my hair, my clothes. He told me I needed to drop ten pounds, and that I looked years older than all my friends.

'He bitched about everything I did. He said I gave the kids too many snacks, and overcooked everything. I bought a new suit for a wedding, and he said it was a waste when I didn't bother to take care of my body.

'It wasn't just me. All our friends noticed how distracted he seemed, and how impatient he was with the kids. Even his mother asked me if I thought he needed to see a doctor, she was so worried about the change in him.

'One afternoon, he came home early from work and said he wanted a divorce. Of course I demanded to know if he was having an affair. He just said, "It's not the point. I wouldn't want you if you were the last woman on Earth." In the end, he broke down and admitted it. It was almost a relief to know I hadn't been imagining things.'

Becky, 34, civil servant

He might seem distracted, and emotionally absent, barely listening when you talk about family issues that should matter to him. He'll forget things; he'll insist he told you something you *know* he hasn't mentioned (he's forgotten it was the Bitch he told, not you) or refer to a movie you haven't seen (he's forgotten he saw it with *her*).

He'll develop a taste for foods you've never known him eat before – sushi, for example. So who introduced him to it? And where's he eating it?

Suddenly he knows about wines.

He's never hungry when he comes home, because he's been taking the Bitch out for a meal, not slaving away at the office like he told you. Or he comes home starving from a supposed business dinner (well, be fair, all that shagging burns a lot of calories).

At weekends, he bitches endlessly about your cooking, and won't touch his favourite steak-and-kidney pie because it's 'fattening'. Since when did he give a shit about his waist-line?

He might go on a health-food kick, announce he's going vegetarian or switch from coffee to herbal tea. He'll ask you to cook foods you've never heard of, or moan because you boil veggies instead of steaming them.

Men are creatures of routine, remember? If his habits change, you should make it your business to know why.

Has he suddenly developed a passion for photography? Or stopped playing golf? If he now undresses in the dark, or wears pyjamas to bed when he used to prefer his birthday suit, he may be hiding scratch marks or love-bites.

Does he close the bathroom door for privacy, when he

used to leave it wide open? Has he stopped wandering around naked in the morning?

He might stop going to church; there's nothing like breaking the seventh commandment to make you feel guilty.

His taste in music, books and films might undergo a radical change, thanks to the new influence in his life. If he starts sporting cowboy boots, *really* worry.

He used to avoid exercise like the plague, but now he's a total gym bunny; or he *says* he is. Who knows where he goes when he says he's working out? Check his gym bag to see if he's ever actually worn his trainers.

Ditto a sudden willingness to take the dog on long walks (is Fido getting fitter or fatter?) or do the weekend shop for you at Sainsbury's. Actually, if he volunteers for that, and he's *not* having an affair, you need to get him checked out by a doctor pronto.

When you drag him on your annual family holiday to the south of France, does he take off his wedding ring 'because his fingers puff up in the heat'? Yeah, whatever. He just doesn't want a tell-tale white band when he removes the ring to cheat.

Has he started smoking again? Or drinking heavily? Check his wallet: has he taken out the photos of you and the kids?

When you go to a new restaurant, one you've never been to before, does the maître d' greet him by name? If he goes out with the 'lads', does he come home with a mood on? (I shouldn't have to tell you what it means if he smells of perfume.)

He could start using words or expressions – especially slang – you've never heard him say before. One girlfriend of mine discovered her husband was having an affair when he started to refer to 'having a cwtch' – pronounced 'kootch' – with the kids at bedtime. It's a Welsh word for cuddle. She'd only ever heard it once before: when she stopped by his office and met his glamorous new secretary . . . who hailed from Cardiff.

He doesn't say 'I love you' any more; or else he says it all the time as a kind of placebo, something he never used to do. He doesn't call you 'darling', just your given name.

He might stop hanging out with his usual friends, who disapprove of his affair, and cultivate new, single ones, whom he won't want you to meet because they know about the Bitch. When you do run into his old friends, they seem nervous or twitchy around you. He's totally lost interest in the house, even though he was filled with enthusiasm for renovating it when you bought it a year or two ago.

If there has been no seismic, life-changing event that you know about – losing his job, for example, or the death of one of his parents – then there's been a seismic, life-changing event that you *don't* know about. Yes, that's right. The Bitch.

Absence makes the prick grow stronger

Finally, unless your man is doing a Boris Becker and fornicating in a restaurant broom cupboard for approximately thirty-five seconds (long enough to father a child, apparently) an affair will require *time*. He can only carve so much from his work day. The rest he steals from you.

He'll have all sorts of new obligations and hobbies that

keep him from home, quite apart from the 'late night at the office, darling'.

Men aren't stupid. Well, they are; but they're also possessed of a low cunning. He'll slip out of the house when you're too busy with the kids to quiz him for details, or pretend he hasn't heard you when you ask. If you insist on coming to Homebase with him 'to pick out a new drill', he'll suddenly change his mind and stay home.

When asked, he'll either be vague about the details of his errand, or give you enough information to write a short novel.

He'll come back from buying a newspaper without the newspaper. He's been to the dentist so often you're starting to wonder if he has three rows of teeth. He says he's jogging, but his weight is going *up*. (All those fancy meals with the Bitch at your expense.)

He seems to disappear from social gatherings for hours at a time; either to phone her or, if she doesn't live too far away, to slip her a quick one.

Patterns. Routines. Habits. *Change.*

Ring my bell

Did I strike a nerve? If this chapter has rung even a few bells and stirred not a little terror in your fragile heart, you need to sift through the evidence very carefully now. You don't want to jump to paranoid conclusions – but nor is it a good idea to take a paddle steamer up Denial. So, in the next chapter, you'll find a helpful little aid: the Bobbitt Quiz. (I don't think I need to explain the genesis of that title.)

But be warned: be *very* sure you're ready for the result.

In a nutshell

Look for:
- Changes in your sex life
- Changes in his appearance
- Phone and communication giveaways
- Unusual work patterns
- Financial clues
- Internet and computer giveaways
- Car clues
- Unfamiliar presents and gifts
- Signs in your home
- Changes in his attitude to you
- Changes in his personality

Remember: when a man leaves his wife, there's always another woman – always!

Chapter Six
The Bobbitt Quiz

I realize this may be a bit of a stretch, given the preceding few chapters, but believe me, I'm not a complete cynic. I accept there *are* innocent explanations for some changes in a man's routine, appearance or habits (though not for the walking-in-on-them-having-sex thing. Sorry). The way the economy's been doing lately, I should think half of us could tick a few of the boxes below.

The key word here is 'few'.

The case for infidelity is often circumstantial, at least in the beginning. Usually, it isn't one single piece of evidence that gives the game away; rather, lots of small things add up to one ugly, big one.

Only you know what's usual for your man. You need to look at the overall picture, put it into context, and decide if two and two make four for *you*.

So do the quiz. Forget what your mother told you: for once, you're allowed to write in a book. But use pencil. You may want to do this quiz more than once, at different times . . . or for different men.

If you tick more than half the boxes in any of the sections

– except the one regarding finances – or you score 60 or more overall, you've got a fairly solid circumstantial case. Certainly enough to get that moral search warrant to dig further.

And remember: he may not be cheating *yet*. He could just be considering an affair, or have met someone to whom he's strongly attracted. You may yet have time to nip it in the bud before it goes any further.

But if you tick more than two or three in the financial section, do not pass Go, and do not collect £200. *He's guilty*.

Sex

1. He's gone off sex ☐
2. He wants more sex ☐
3. He can't get an erection ☐
4. The old dog has some new tricks ☐
5. The sex is (newly) crap ☐
6. He's stopped kissing you/looking into your eyes, especially during sex ☐
7. You find a secret stash of porn for the first time ☐
8. You find condoms when you don't use them ☐
9. He insists you/he start using birth control ☐
10. You find lipstick on his underpants or a girl in his bed ☐

Ties

1. He smartens up his wardrobe ☐
2. He changes his style, dumping the stonewashed jeans and going low-rise ☐

3. He gets all dressed up for a 'night out with the boys' ☐
4. He changes his type of underwear ☐
5. He won't let you shop for him ☐
6. He covers up his grey ☐
7. He seems to live in front of the bathroom mirror ☐
8. He trades in his British snaggle teeth for a dazzling Hollywood smile ☐
9. He turns from couch potato to fitness fanatic overnight ☐
10. He loses weight and becomes a vegan (no, not Mr Spock, Mr Lentil) ☐

Guilty as charged

1. You get a significant number of hang-ups, wrong numbers and blocked calls ☐
2. An unknown number recurs frequently on your phone bill ☐
3. He moves his phone charger somewhere private ☐
4. He deletes his call history and messages ☐
5. Male first names you don't know crop up in his address book ☐
6. He takes calls in private, whispers into the phone and checks to see where you are ☐
7. He always seems to be hanging up the phone when you walk into a room ☐
8. He never goes anywhere without his mobile ☐
9. You find he has a mobile you didn't know existed ☐
10. A woman answers when you press Redial or 1471 ☐

No work and all play

1. He works late at/goes in early to the office ☐
2. There's a sudden increase in business trips or entertaining without a change in job ☐
3. He goes cool on you socializing with anyone at his office ☐
4. His colleagues are nervous when you're around ☐
5. You get different stories from different people at his office when you try to track him down (a clear sign they're covering for him) ☐
6. Any signs that he's a family man have disappeared from his office ☐
7. He claims he's working overtime, but he doesn't seem to earn any more ☐
8. He calls you late and says he's at work – but when you call back with something you'd forgotten to tell him, nobody answers ☐
9. He *always* calls you morning and early evening when he's away ☐
10. His business trips take a day or two longer than they used to ☐

Money makes the Bitch come round

1. He works 'overtime', but it doesn't show up in his salary ☐
2. He switches the payment of his salary from your joint account to another of his choosing ☐
3. You're struggling financially, and it's not (all) the City boys' fault ☐

4. He withdraws significant sums of cash from your account ☐
5. He starts playing the tight-wad at home ☐
6. He tries to make you get a job ☐
7. Restaurant and other unexplained bills show up on his credit card ☐
8. He takes out a new credit card and doesn't tell you ☐
9. You find paperwork for bank or savings accounts you didn't know about ☐
10. He plays fast and loose with your assets so that you can't keep track of them ☐

Virtually yours

1. He stays up late at night 'working' on the computer ☐
2. He closes his laptop when you walk in the room ☐
3. Over-familiar instant messages pop up on his screen ☐
4. He never leaves his laptop at home any more ☐
5. He sets up a new email account ☐
6. He changes his password frequently ☐
7. He puts his BlackBerry on vibrate so you don't know when he's getting messages ☐
8. You find incriminating or suggestive emails to or from him ☐
9. He deletes his online history ☐
10. He waits until he's alone to check and reply to his messages ☐

Come on, baby, drive my car

1. His car smells of cigarettes or an unfamiliar perfume ☐
2. You find condoms in the glove compartment ☐
3. Whenever you go to the 'emergency' box of wet wipes you keep in the car for the kids, it's empty ☐
4. He keeps a blanket or change of clothes in the boot ☐
5. Every time you get in the car, you have to adjust the passenger seat ☐
6. The radio is tuned to Country & Western, and he's a rabid Radio 4 man ☐
7. You find a CD you don't recognize in the sound system ☐
8. The passenger mirror is left down (from when she reapplied her lippy) ☐
9. He says he went to Birmingham on business, but the sat-nav is programmed to a hotel in Kent ☐
10. You get a parking ticket from a borough the other end of the country when he's not supposed to have been away ☐

The gift that keeps giving

1. He starts wearing novelty ties or socks (and you didn't buy them) ☐
2. He displays an expensive new watch, but there's no sign of payment for it on any of your credit-card statements ☐

3. He suddenly showers you with gifts 'because you're you' ☐
4. He tells you to 'buy something pretty' for your birthday, instead of choosing it himself ☐
5. He gives you a set of cheap padded coat hangers for Christmas ☐
6. He doesn't bother to buy you anything ☐
7. He splashes out and buys you a wildly expensive piece of jewellery ☐
8. He remembers Valentine's Day for the first time since you've known him ☐
9. You find a receipt for a big bottle of your favourite perfume, but he never gives it to you ☐
10. You stumble across a pretty lingerie set at the back of his wardrobe that you expect to turn up in your Christmas stocking – and it doesn't ☐

Home is where the tart is

1. The champagne glasses were used while you were away ☐
2. There are cigarette butts in the fireplace ☐
3. There's an unfamiliar bottle of shampoo in the shower ☐
4. He's changed the sheets while you were staying at your mother's ☐
5. The towels are in the wrong place in the airing cupboard ☐
6. You find stubs for a movie you didn't go to in his pocket ☐
7. There's a key you don't recognize on his keyring ☐

8. His desk diary is filled with cryptic notes ☐
9. Sade is in the CD player ☐
10. The cable bill shows a chick-flick rom-com movie selection from when you were out of town ☐

I love you too

1. He's unusually irritable, impatient or angry with you ☐
2. He criticizes you constantly, and puts you down in front of other people ☐
3. He interrupts you when you try to talk to him, answers in monosyllables or gives you the silent treatment ☐
4. He doesn't want to do any of the things you once enjoyed doing together ☐
5. When you come into a room, he leaves it ☐
6. He avoids any kind of physical contact, from holding hands to kissing ☐
7. He no longer calls you by your pet name ☐
8. He seems preoccupied, and is constantly forgetful ☐
9. He encourages you to go out and do things with other people ☐
10. He accuses you of cheating on him ☐

When did you last see your husband?

1. He seems to have been lobotomized and turned into a totally different person ☐
2. He's unusually grumpy and withdrawn ☐
3. He's full of the joys of spring for no apparent reason ☐

4. He develops a passion for sushi ☐
5. Suddenly he can't stand your shepherd's pie ☐
6. He's never hungry when he comes home ☐
7. He suddenly can't get enough of the tennis club ☐
8. He undresses in the dark when he used to walk around naked ☐
9. He stops going to church ☐
10. His taste in books, music and films changes dramatically ☐
11. He starts living at the gym ☐
12. He takes up hobbies that mean he's out of the house for long periods ☐
13. He starts smoking ☐
14. He stops saying 'I love you' or using endearments towards you ☐
15. He takes you to a 'new place in town' and every-one seems to know him ☐
16. He uses words or expressions, especially slang, he's never used before ☐
17. He drops his old friends for new ones you never meet ☐
18. He loses interest in anything long-term: doing up the house, next summer's holiday, a new car ☐
19. He runs an errand – but forgets to pick up what-ever he went out for ☐
20. He disappears for long periods of time from social gatherings ☐

Scoring

If you ticked more than half the boxes in any section (except Money makes the Bitch come round): it doesn't look good

More than 60/120 overall: ditto

More than 3/10 in Money makes the Bitch come round: take the bastard down

Chapter Seven
Not All Affairs are Equal

So, you've woken up to the threat that all women pose to your happiness. You've watched. You've snooped. You've done the Bobbitt Quiz. And now you know for certain: he's having an affair.

Before we go any further, let me make one thing clear. Men who cheat are pathetic, lying bastards.

Sorry, I take that back. What I *meant* to say was that they're pathetic, lying, weak, useless, feeble, feckless, incompetent, spineless, worthless, deceitful, reptilian, dishonest, two-faced, yellow-bellied, double-dealing, mendacious, duplicitous, cowardly, gutless, craven, lily-livered, pusillanimous, disloyal, treacherous, traitorous, cruel, heartless, callous, fraudulent, corrupt, unfair, double-crossing, insincere, unfaithful, perfidious, underhand, shifty, shitty, unfeeling, devious, faithless, wretched, sad, fickle, swindling, unreliable, untrustworthy, shabby, shit-bag, ratfink, *bastardy* bastards with bells on.

So. Any man who screws around is Not A Nice Person. I think we're clear on that. But. *But.* It's important to recognize there are different types of infidelity; and different types of Infidels. I'm probably traducing some fundamentalist feminist dogma by saying this, but not all affairs are equal.

Before you think I'm going soft on adultery, or the causes of adultery, let me state here and now: *cheating is cheating*, plain and simple. Debating the degree of the fucker's treachery is a little like discussing how pregnant you are. There's absolutely *no excuse* for infidelity.

None.

Boys, I don't care if your girlfriend is a crack-addicted bisexual lush with a split personality, vaginal yeast infection and chronic halitosis: going out and bedding someone else doesn't fix *any*thing. If you really need to shoot your wad that badly, go jerk off in the bathroom.

(And no, her having a crush on Jonathan Ross is *not* a mitigating factor, as one of my male interviewees suggested. Though I can see why he thought it should be.)

When a woman has just found out her man has been playing hide-the-sausage with someone else, she doesn't usually care about the precise classification of his betrayal. It's as much as she can manage just to stand upright.

You feel as if you've been punched in the gut. You can't breathe, you can't eat, you can't sleep. You cry so much, you can't imagine there are any more tears left. You can't believe how much it hurts. *Physically* hurts: every bone and joint and tendon and muscle aches, as if you've been hit by a lorry and left for dead.

I know, because I've been there. I know how sick and disorientated you feel. How confused and lost you are. At this precise moment, you don't want to know *why* the man who swore he'd love you for ever has gone out and had sex with another woman. Your world has just ended. What does it matter?

It matters. Understanding what sort of affair this is, and why he had it, will be crucial in determining how you survive and come back from this.

Some women I spoke to (usually the v. v. posh ones; taking a mistress to relieve one's wife of the 'marriage debt' seems almost *expected* amongst the upper classes) said they could forgive a quick roll in the hay as long as no real emotions were involved. Others (those of us who buy our furniture, rather than inherit it) felt it'd be more acceptable, and somehow less insulting, if their husband or boyfriend cheated because he fancied himself madly in love.

Personally, I think it's a bit like Death Row inmates debating the merits of hanging versus the electric chair.

But whatever your particular view, you do need to know into which category of Infidel your man falls, because it will affect the way you annihilate his Bitch.

She slipped and fell on my prick

Let's start with the basic model: your common-or-garden Accidental Adulterer.

This dim-witted booby is the epitome of carelessness. He didn't fall in love ('Whatever that means': Prince Charles, 1981), or deliberately take a lover because he likes the taste of new pussy. No, this nincompoop had an affair by mistake. 'She slipped and fell on my prick, m'lud. No, honest. It was an *accident*.'

Pitiful, isn't it?

I don't know about you, but on balance I think I'd rather my man had the balls (if you'll excuse the pun) to go out and cheat on purpose.

The Accidental Adulterer is weak-willed, craven and easily tempted. He's the one any Bitch worthy of the name can spot in a hotel bar at a hundred paces.

He doesn't set out to have an affair – at least, not *consciously*. He doesn't really want to leave his wife, his kids, his three square meals and nice semi in the 'burbs, and end up stuck in a crappy bedsit with a girl who's too young to have heard of Pink Floyd, washing his own socks and eating Pot Noodles. He *loves* his wife, dammit. He doesn't want anything to change.

> 'When Lisa showed an interest in me at work, I didn't resist, thinking initially I was just flirting. But somehow one thing led to another, and pretty soon I was engulfed in an affair I didn't really want, and certainly hadn't planned. Every time I said I wanted to end it, she threatened to tell my wife. I was trapped. In the end, I couldn't stand the tension – I told my wife myself. She left me.'
>
> *Jason, 38, restaurant manager*

But yeah, he's bored. He doesn't know where the slim, carefree, sexy girl he married has gone. (She's still there, you prick; at least, what's left of her after she's finished schlepping after you and the kids, cooking, cleaning, doing the school run, the laundry, the Christmas shopping, putting up shelves and taking down wallpaper – we're not having it all, stupid, we're *doing* it all) – organizing school raffles and your mother's birthday party, dropping your son off at football and your daughter at ballet, planning next summer's holiday, booking the dentist, cancelling the hairdresser –

seriously, who has the time? – taking the dog to the vet, the bottles to the recycling centre and the baby to the paediatrician. And that's *just in one day*. You *really* think she's got the energy to come home and get trussed up in the tacky, itchy, too-small lace teddy you bought her last Christmas?)

But boyo here just doesn't get it. As far as he's concerned, if she can't shimmy down the stairs in thigh-high stiletto boots and a leather catsuit twice a week, she's let herself go.

You can almost see the little speech bubbles over his head as he trails his wife morosely around the supermarket, can't you?

It's not that I don't love her. We still get along OK. She scrubs up pretty well when she makes the effort. But she's put a bit of weight on recently, even she'd admit that, yeah? She used to wear all these hot mini-skirts, but these days, she seems to live in that bloody grey tracksuit . . .

(Head swivels, as if on stick, as girl in skimpy top walks past.)

She's always so busy worrying about the kids, and work, and money. I swear she doesn't notice I'm there half the time. I can't remember the last time we had sex—

(Jumps as wife digs him in ribs for drooling.)

There's got to be more to life than this. We got together when we were really young; I can't help wondering if I'm missing something, especially when the lads go on about their sexploits at the weekend. OK, yeah, I'll admit I'm curious what it'd be like to fuck someone new after all this time. Especially when that girl at the King's Arms smiles at me and bends over so I can see right down her top. Little bitch never even bothers with a bra . . .

So he loves his wife, but maybe he's not *in love* with her

any more. And it's at this ripe moment that he falls over an Opportunity.

> Dan: 'I don't think having dinner with anybody is a crime.'
> Alex: 'Not yet.'
>
> **Fatal Attraction**

Consequences? What consequences?

Maybe it happens through work; put any man with a pulse alone in a hotel room far away from home and vigilant cats, and the mice will play.

Perhaps she's someone he's known for years, and thought safe to arrange to meet for a drink when he bumped into her by chance. (Has he never seen *When Harry Met Sally*? Men and women can't be friends, because the sex part always gets in the way, remember?)

Office parties are particularly deadly: it's the combination of holiday high and alcohol. Little wonder it's a breeding ground for indiscretion. Like a drunk driver whose judgement is so clouded he still thinks it safe to get behind the wheel after seventeen beers, he's incapable of thinking through the consequences of his actions when he snogs the praying mantis from HR. When he wakes up in her bed the next morning with a raging hangover and a bellyful of regret and says it 'just happened', as far as he's concerned, it *did*.

'Louise and I went way back. She dated my brother for a while, but I honestly never thought of her in that sense; to me she was just one of the boys. We hung out, shot pool, but it was never anything more serious. She didn't show the slightest interest in me as anything other than a friend.

'Over the years we lost touch, and then last Christmas we ran into each other in Asda. We swapped numbers, but I didn't really think any more about it until she rang me out of the blue about a month later. She was in my neck of the woods and wondered if I wanted to meet up for a drink. I thought it'd be nice to catch up, and things had been a bit fraught at home recently – my wife, Kathy, and I had been trying for a baby for quite a while and things were pretty tense.

'We both had quite a lot to drink, and when she invited me back to her place, I was flattered. The sex was fine, but as soon as I sobered up, I felt like a total shit. I realized Louise had planned it all, and I fell for it like a total sucker. I love Kathy, and would never want to hurt her. She'd kill me if she found out, and I don't blame her. I can't believe I've been so stupid.'

Peter, 35, marketing director

Some men simply don't know how to Just Say No. The male of the species isn't programmed to decline sex when it's proffered.

An Accidental Adulterer often considers himself perfectly content with the ways things are at home; the last thing he expects is to have an affair, but then a Bitch comes along and offers herself on a plate. Somehow he feels it would be a reflection on his manhood – and his manners – to decline.

Other men get swept along by the sheer force of peer pressure: everyone else is screwing around, so if they want to be one of the boys, maybe they should too.

When I was in my early twenties, I worked as a producer at ITN for four years. I travelled all over the world with reporters and TV crews, almost all of whom were married or in long-term relationships, and almost all of whom regularly cheated on their wives and girlfriends.

(Several of them are now well-known household names and are still happily married to the same wives, as far as I know; hence my uncharacteristic discretion.)

One correspondent was such a player I had no idea he was even married for the first year I worked with him. He escorted a parade of pretty girls to awards ceremonies and company functions; I was genuinely shocked when I discovered he had a wife stowed out of sight somewhere in the country.

Even otherwise-decent, happily married men suddenly turned into Jack the Lad when they were on the road. There they'd be, holed up in some foreign hotel, the wife safely stashed at home with the kids. The cameraman and producer would be picking up totty left and right; and then there'd turn out to be one girl spare, sitting on the banquette making bedroom eyes in his direction. What happens in Bosnia stays in Bosnia, right?

I remember one young reporter who plainly adored his wife. They'd been married less than a year and he talked about her constantly. Every time he went on the road, his camera crew took the piss out of him for going to bed early and alone. Finally, after one drink and one ribbing too many, he ended up in bed with a news groupie. The next morning, I saw him sobbing his eyes out in a corner of the hotel lobby.

He left ITN soon afterwards to work in local government. Much safer.

Danger is famously a great aphrodisiac. In the crucible of a war zone, when you never know if any day will be your last, impulses that would otherwise fade in an instant are hothoused out of all recognition. (Just ask the pretty English girls who ended the Second World War with a squalling American souvenir.)

But let's put the excuses aside. My point is: Accidental Adulterers are not generally wicked and irredeemable Philanderers. They're weak, yes; stupid, reckless even – but they don't consciously set out to betray their wives. Usually, they feel pretty bloody awful about it afterwards, and in most cases don't want to repeat the experience. Their first instinct is to run a mile from the woman involved – something that's not always possible if she's a work colleague or friend of the family.

> Alex: 'What am I supposed to do? You won't answer my calls, you change your number . . . I'm not going to be ignored, Dan!'
>
> *Fatal Attraction*

None of this lessens the impact or pain for you if you discover what your husband or boyfriend has been up to. There are a number of ways to fight back, which I'll talk about in detail later; though some women would argue that it's not up for debate, since even one mistake is inexcusable. Which is fine, as long as you can live up to the same unforgiving standards.

The real trick, of course, is to make sure it doesn't happen in the first place. Of which more later.

---

5 things an Accidental Adulterer will never say

1. **Of course I could have helped it!**
2. **I did it on purpose**
3. **It's my fault**
4. **It didn't just happen, I went round to her place with malice aforethought**
5. **It wasn't about you or our marriage, it was about me**

Remind me: what's your name?

Some men are like accident blackspots. These unfortunate bedroom mishaps *will* keep happening to them. Perhaps their groins should be sectioned off by cones.

A man who has multiple one-night stands is half hapless Accidental Adulterer – which is how they often start their sleazy careers – and half Philanderer, which, unless you stop him, is where he may end up.

He doesn't fall in love or get involved – most of the time, he doesn't even catch their names – and certainly wouldn't classify what he does as an *affair*. For him, sex has become a basic bodily function, of no more moment than sneezing or yawning, to be performed as often as possible with any willing accomplice.

The principle difference between him and a Philanderer is that he's still in denial. Even though he keeps waking up between other women's thighs, he never has any idea how he ended up there, because he thinks he's 'perfectly happy' at home.

Unlike our Accidental Adulterer, however, who may truly love his wife, Mr One Night Stand is kidding himself. To mis-quote the inimitable Oscar again: to have one fling may be regarded as a misfortune; to have two looks like carelessness.

Repeatedly having women fall on your sword is an addic-tion like any other (which, by the way, *doesn't mean they can't help it*). The quality of the marriage isn't the problem; it's the quality of the man you're married to.

'Leave him. It's that simple. Move on and don't live in hope. That's easy for me to say and I know that if you love someone, and especially if you have young kids, it's not easy, but it really is best, for you and for your kids. File for divorce and make a break. He's not coming back and if he does, he'll do it again. You need to find the strength to send him away again.'

The English Courtesan,
www.englishcourtesan.blogspot.com

Men who flit from one bed to the next without making any real connection with the women they're fucking may seem cocky and confident, but deep down, they believe they're inadequate shits (so they've got that right, then). When they get into another girl's knickers, it gives them an instant high, making them feel powerful, attractive and invincible.

But, like any other addiction, they need a hit more and more often, until eventually it controls them, rather than the other way round. They may not realize they're doing it, but these men are already looking for the next conquest even as they tumble out of the last girl's bed and zip up their flies.

Unlike Accidental Adulterers, a man who has serial flings is *not* fundamentally happy, with himself, his wife or his marriage. And unless he chooses to go cold turkey and break himself of the habit, nothing you can do or say will change him.

What really triggers the addiction in the first place, other than feeling crap about himself? Well, it can be as simple as an accidental shag that goes horribly *right*, i.e. he doesn't get caught, and once the fear has passed, doesn't really feel guilty (or, at least, not guilty enough). So, sooner or later, he 'slips up' again. And again.

Or it may be precipitated by some sort of stress: turning forty's a favourite. It doesn't have to be a negative stress, though; a new baby is another sure-fire hit. Since *you're* the one with heartburn, stretchmarks, piles, varicose veins, toes you haven't seen for six months and boobs the size of Guernsey, this has always struck me as a bit rich. But it happens more often than you might think, so there we are.

Buying a house, getting a promotion, losing a parent: basically, anything that suggests maturity, responsibility, commitment, and all those other scary words that give men the willies.

Different men deal with stress in different ways, and

while we'd all rather our boyfriends and husbands got a funny twitch or developed a mild drinking problem instead of leaping into bed with any slapper who bats her eyelashes at him, if you've got a stress flinger, you can either (a) leave him, (b) learn to head his crises off at the pass, or (c) give him the number of a nice clean call-girl.

It's terminal, Mrs Jones

If Mr One Night Stand doesn't end up buried beneath the patio while his widow lives it up in Magaluf on the life insurance, sooner or later he'll quietly admit to himself that he's thoroughly enjoying having his cake and eating it, and graduate to fully fledged Philanderer.

Philanderers are tough ones to beat. Kind of like the liver cancer of the Adultery Club: by the time you find out you've got it, it's almost always too late.

The good news (on a par with 'I'm afraid it's terminal, Mrs Jones, but think how much weight you're going to lose!') is that usually Philanderers will not leave you.

They're also different from Accidental Adulterers in one crucial respect: the concept of self-doubt is utterly incomprehensible to them. Basically, they think they're the dog's bollocks. They're convinced they've got it made, and that every other man would behave the same way they do, given half a chance.

Whilst our Accidental Adulterer feels shitty about cheating on his wife, Casanova here is blissfully unaware of his faults, and loving life.

Philanderers don't believe in marriage, monogamy or fidelity;

they would never give a woman the measure of control over them that inevitably comes with genuine feelings of love.

They may pride themselves on being lovers of women, but in fact they *hate* and *fear* them; they seduce women to humiliate and tame them. As far as Casanova is concerned, women are inferior – as evidenced by their pathetic willingness to fall into bed with him, of course – and exist primarily to serve men, especially in the bedroom.

Even those who genuinely believe they like women are still unable to think of or treat them as equals; like Bond girls, they are interchangeable and replaceable. Philanderers like women the way a cat likes a mouse.

Philanderers are not cute. They are *not* charming, wayward boys who can't help themselves. They are dangerous, dead inside, predatory in their pathology.

It goes beyond deceit. Somebody who behaves with such a total indifference to any morality must have a strong sense that it is his 'right' so to do. And that makes for a lethally destructive person.

And yet we're addicted to them, aren't we? The Bad Boys. We always think we can change them, that we can be the one to tame them through the (cue Jennifer Rush) Power of Love.

It really is ridiculous, isn't it? Why do we go looking for a bastard we can reform when we could pick a man who's already a decent guy?

It's back to the caves and the alpha-male thing, I'm afraid. Evolution told men to scatter their seed far and wide, to propagate their genes and the species; and it programmed women to want the man at the top of the pack, the man everyone else craved too.

'I've never been faithful to my wife, even before we married. We've been together eighteen years and still have sex at least once a day, and it's brilliant but predictable. I know how to turn on my wife. Discovering how to turn on a new partner is a drug. I got a bit bored of sex at home and I wanted some fresh pussy, so I started sleeping with younger women whose arses were firmer and tits were standing up more. That was a bit of a drug, too. Young skin smells different and I kind of got addicted to the freshness of young women's bodies.

'I try to see my girlfriends over lunch so I don't have to make up excuses to my wife. I pick girls who have flats close to the office so that I can get round there for an hour of hot sex then shower and get back to work. Occasionally, if there's a work function, I will make an appearance and then head round to a girlfriend's flat and spend two or three hours in bed till about one or two a.m. and then go home.

'I always make it clear I'm not leaving my wife because I refuse to be a stay-away dad. I may be a crap husband but I am a good dad and I would hate my kids to get caught in the crossfire of a divorce.

'I think I will be faithful when I get bored of the intrigue and the stress of it all. And I know there will come a day not too far off when some young woman tells me I am a dirty old man and then I will retire from womanizing in embarrassment.

'If I didn't have kids I would probably jack the wife in and spend the rest of my forties at least trying to fuck as many twenty-five-to-thirty-five-year-olds as I could manage. Then I'd remarry the wife.'

Scott, 43, construction manager

A recent study by American researchers discovered women like nothing better than to bag a selfish, deceitful, self-obsessed narcissist. And surprise, surprise, men like nothing better than using these three traits – catchily dubbed the 'Dark Triad' by geeks with an eye to the head-lines and a grant for their next edge-of-your-seat research paper: 'Do Women Prefer a Diamond Ring to a Poke in the Eye?' – to get us in the sack.

Lie, you bugger, lie!

The Dark Triad (which, contrary to what you might think, actually has nothing to do with either the Chinese Mafia or a man who's incredibly well hung; that's a *tripod*) comprises three seductive attributes: he has to be (a) a good liar; (b) totally selfish; and (c) prone to the kind of rash, impulsive behaviour that cares little for the consequences.

The scientists thus define the ultimate bastard as James Bond. Which brings us back to Daniel Craig again (really, any excuse will do). Like Strawberry Fields in *Quantum of Solace*, we're all *very* cross with ourselves as we let him kiss his way seductively up our spines.

Bad Boy addiction isn't just a predilection of the West, either. Another team of excited researchers (seriously, how do these people submit their grant applications with a straight face?) found that the phenomenon of the 'bastard junkie' was evident across different countries and different cultures. Well, knock me down with a feather and call me Maisie.

What was it that gave it away, doctor? All those myths and legends and books and plays and films, crammed to bursting with seductive bastards from Casanova, Lothario and Don Juan – yes, the clue is in the eponym – to Heathcliff, Rhett Butler and *Sex and the City*'s Mr Big? Surely not.

Apparently, there are also more bastards around these days, too; literally and figuratively. According to the scientists, all that plentiful casual sex means they've been passing on those dodgy genes for generations, which is why the nice guys are getting harder to find. (Yeah, right. And I'm Mother Teresa. The real reason there are fewer nice guys is because they've finally cottoned on to the fact that the Bad Boys are the ones getting all the sex.)

Not that they really have to lie to us at all. We're only too happy to lie to ourselves on their behalf.

We tell ourselves that beneath the uncaring, heartless exterior is a vulnerable Mr Darcy, struggling with the intensity and unfamiliarity of his true feelings. He only behaves badly because he's damaged, we sigh. He's hard to read because he's 'deep'. He stands us up, lets us down and fails us again and again because he's a 'free spirit'. All he really needs is the love of a good woman.

How stupid are we?

When he says he's not worth it, he's *telling the truth*. He behaves badly because he *can*. He's not hard to read at all: we just don't like what he's telling us. He lets us down because he's a fucking bastard, and the more good women love him, the worse he's going to behave.

Oh, but they're so seductive, these charming heartbreakers! My Philanderer (yes, yes, I had one too, of course I did: don't we all? The man who truly broke your heart with his sweet smile and empty promises) was thoughtful, witty, urbane, sexy, intelligent, tender, charismatic: in short, *mesmerizing*. He did more than make me laugh; he raised my game and made me witty in return. *I* made *him* laugh. With him, I was sparkling and vivacious and desirable. I didn't just fall in love with him; I fell in love with *me*.

He didn't try to get me into bed; he was far too clever for that. No, he seduced me into seducing him. And this brings me to the other crucial difference between Mr One Night Stand and a Philanderer: with the latter, *it's not all about the sex*.

He wants to seduce you, yes; but the seduction doesn't have to be physical. In fact, these days, with women treating sex like a game of tennis in the same way men have done for centuries, it can be hard to know who's using whom in the bedroom. But get a woman to fall in love with you . . . now that *is* a power trip.

Consider this email:

There's no subtle way to say this, so I'm just going to jump in.

I think of you constantly. I wonder where you are and what you're saying, who you're with and how you're looking at them. Is it the same way you look at me? Are you thinking about me? What are you thinking? Did you change your mind? When are you going to call me? Do you still want to see me? Do you enjoy being with me?

After leaving you I dissect the conversations we had. Could I have said something differently? Could I have been funnier? Did she understand what I meant? Could she have taken

that the wrong way? Was I being too vague? Too
ridiculous? Too quirky?!

I don't fully understand what's happening in my
mind. The only things I know for sure are that
I'm simply crazy about you and that I want to be
with you now.

The feel of your skin and your breath on my
cheek. The smile on my face when I'm with you.
When we kiss and seem to be surviving on each
other's breath. Your smell. The tip of your
tongue on my ear, my skin, my chest. You smiling
at me and looking into my eyes and even smiling
at me with yours. Warmth. Your skin against
mine. My cheek against your stomach. The kisses
that neither start nor finish, that just happen.

Knowing my own ability to avoid subjects that
are too intense, too personal or that I just
don't want to answer, I have to say that I have
never been so thoroughly seduced and mesmerized
in my life.

Masterful, isn't it? Toxic, of course, but masterful.

As an opening seduction salvo, which this email was, it
hits every button. You're different, it says. You'll be the one
to change me, to save me from myself. I'm vulnerable. Only
with you can I open up and tell you things I've never told
anyone before.

What really confuses our inbuilt bullshit detectors,
of course, is that when a Philanderer says these things,
he often means them. *At the time.* What he fails to mention, of course, is that the moment we succumb to his

charms and fall in love with him, he'll instantly cool.

(You know who you are.)

Many are powerful, successful, good-looking men. Just open any celebrity glossy, close your eyes and stab the page. You'll hit one. They know they've got the pick of the tribe, with women falling over themselves to ally themselves to the leader of the pack. Naturally, this sort of power is not good for any man. Often men who're able to have any woman they choose lose respect for *all* women.

Men need challenges. It's a fundamental law of nature: they want what they can't have. They're drawn to bitches (small 'b') in precisely the same way women are drawn to bastards.

Men need to know you're unavailable in a subtle but significant sense; which has nothing to do with your *actual* availability. You can even be married to a man and still maintain a degree of unattainability with him. Forget the deluded tree huggers who insist that sharing every nook and cranny of your psyche is the recipe for a long and happy marriage. It's actually a go-directly-to-jail short-cut to the divorce court.

But of this, more later. For now, the key point to remember is that Philanderers don't change.

Say it again with me: *Philanderers don't change.*

There is a chance – a very *slim* chance – that he may get too old, too tired or too poor to cheat any more; but I wouldn't hold my breath.

(A doctor friend of mine works on a geriatric ward. She says that if she had a quid for every time she's been goosed by an octogenarian, she could afford to retire to the Caribbean and pick up a twenty-two-year-old stud muffin herself.)

If you're saddled with a Philanderer, you have three choices: (a) learn to live with his infidelity; (b) divorce him and take him to the cleaners (see Chapter Twelve: Don't Get Mad, Get Diamonds); or (c) do a Lorena Bobbitt and cut off his willy.*

10 really, really true, I swear, this-isn't-just-a-line philandering lines

1. We haven't slept together since Kitty/Josh/the triplets were born
2. We practically lead separate lives
3. I love her, but I'm not in love with her
4. I love her the way I love my best friend or my sister
5. I'm moving out as soon as the youngest is at nursery/Eton/Oxbridge/medical school/a retirement home
6. We're divorced in all but name
7. I've never felt like this before
8. When I'm with her, I only think of you
9. I can't imagine life without you
10. My wife doesn't get me. (Even Philanderers appreciate that the classic 'My wife doesn't understand me' is a little threadbare)

*This is another one of those literary hyperbole things. The author in no way advocates the removal of body parts as a solution to a man's chronic inability to keep it in his trousers, however tempting it may seem at times. Please do not try this at home.

PEA soup

You might think that having a husband who screws anything that moves is, maritally, the worst that can happen, other than being married to one of the dark triad of Dr Crippen, Ted Bundy and Hannibal Lecter.

You'd be wrong.

The road to Hell is paved with good intentions. And a well-meaning, 'honourable' idiot who fancies himself in love can do far more damage than a philandering bastard on his worst day.

As we've discussed, Accidental Adulterers and Philanderers are very unlikely to leave you. They know which side their bread is buttered, and are often perfectly happy being married to you, either because (a) they love you, (b) they can't afford an expensive divorce, or (c) no one else can make bread-and-butter pudding the way you do. (*You* may decide to throw the cheating fucker out on his ear and/or lace the pudding with arsenic, of course, but that's another matter.)

When men fall in love: *that's* when affairs become dangerous. The women they fall for are the Bitches you have to watch, the ones who want to steal your man, rather than borrow him when you're not playing with him and promise to put him back.

It's a chemistry thing. When we meet someone we fancy, our brains are flooded with an amphetamine-type hormone called phenylethylamine (PEA). PEA creates the sense of euphoria, excitement, sleeplessness and giddiness associated with being 'in love'. But the body's defence mechanism then reacts by producing endorphins to calm us down, a process that can take weeks or months. It averages two years and *never* lasts longer than four. Which means that, sooner or later, *everyone falls out of love again.*

This doesn't have to be a bad thing. In an ideal world, infatuation (which is what 'in love' really means) is replaced by grown-up love. *Real* love. The kind of love that *isn't* blind, that sees all your flaws and warts, and doesn't flinch, but becomes the stronger for it.

The trouble is, as we all know, most men have trouble doing grown-up *any*thing, let alone grown-up love.

Being in love – infatuation – is a kind of insanity. Reason, judgement, dignity, logic, duty, caution, honour, loyalty: all are thrown out of the window. Such lovers are consumed less by love than by the sheer intensity of their feelings, which they fondly imagine to be unique to them, and an excuse for all sorts of deceitful, despicable behaviour, including the aforementioned nonsense in the classifieds every February.

This is the kind of obsession that leads men to risk everything: life, country, fortune and family. Paris started the Trojan Wars when he fell for Helen and pinched her from her husband, Menelaus, the King of Sparta. Henry VIII broke with Rome and the Pope, dissolved the monasteries, founded the Church of England, beheaded half his court and bastardized his daughter in order to free himself of the old pussy he no longer fancied, Catherine of Aragon, and marry his new pussy, Anne Boleyn. It took him nearly ten years to get what he wanted; barely three years later, he accused Anne of incest, adultery and witchcraft and cut off her head, so he could move on to his new love, who became wife number three. See what I mean about the four-year rule? If ever a girl ended up in the PEA soup, it was Anne.

(A shout-out here to one of the great put-downs of history – Christina of Denmark, the Duchess of Milan, who at sixteen refused to marry Henry VIII after the death of his third wife in childbirth: 'If I had two heads,' quoth the little minx, 'one should be at the King of England's disposal.')

More recently, Edward VIII gave up the crown of England and went into exile as the Duke of Windsor for love of his American divorcee, Wallis Simpson. Our dread monarchs aren't what they were. Henry VIII would have laughed his codpiece off at the thought of abdicating for anyone. Off with their heads!

'I might as well have stayed married'

The litany of infatuated middle-aged men who abandon their wives, along with any semblance of credibility, dignity and respect, for a floozie half their age is biblical in scope.

Such affairs are reckless, passionate, intense – and utterly unrealistic.

Usually, when you meet someone and get the hots for them (sorry, 'fall in love'), those initial, can't-live-without-you feelings develop into a deeper love; or they dissipate, and the relationship dies a natural death.

But when you have an affair, time stands still. The entire relationship is freeze-dried. You're enveloped in a bubble that's secret by its very nature; no daylight is able to enter and illuminate any flaws or weaknesses in the beloved. It's easy to maintain your illusions. You romanticize. You see your lover as perfect; your 'soulmate' (one of the most pernicious and ludicrous terms in the English language).

The reality is that you don't actually know them at all. And because your affair never puts them to the test, the infatuation continues indefinitely.

The truly sad thing is that a marriage and family may be ripped apart, and children left broken-hearted and bereft, for the sake of this transient passion; and yet all too often the new relationship fizzles out the moment it emerges into the pitiless light of day.

Six years ago, an acquaintance of mine left his South African wife, who was four months pregnant, and their two young children, for a woman ten years his junior. His distraught wife fled back to Johannesburg with the boys, but for Dominic, sacrificing regular access to his children was apparently a price worth paying.

'It kills me that I'll only see them once a year, but I'd do anything to be with Maggie,' he told me at the time. 'We have this amazing connection, it's like I've known her all my life. The sex is incredible. She's sexy, funny and so outgoing – all Kristal ever wanted to do was stay home with the kids. Maggie's my soulmate. She's The One.'

Three months ago, we ran into each other while covering a story in New York for our respective newspapers. I hadn't seen him in five years, and was stunned by the change in him. He looked ten years older, and had gained weight and lost hair, but what really surprised me was the palpable air of disappointment that hung about him like a damp shroud.

'Maggie and I have nothing in common,' he complained. 'All she wants to do is party. I can't keep up, and to be honest I don't want to. We don't like the same people or even the same music. We hardly ever have sex any more. I feel such an idiot. I tore my family apart, my kids won't even speak to me, and I'm right back to square one, stuck with a wife I can't even have a conversation with. I might as well have stayed married to Kristal.'

It was hard to be sympathetic, given the appalling way he'd treated his pregnant wife. The poor girl hadn't known what hit her when Dominic abandoned her without a word of explanation, sending her a text to tell her he wanted a divorce.

(Seriously. In what parallel dimension is it *ever* acceptable to end a marriage via fax or text?)

In the past six years, however, Kristal had rebuilt her life in South Africa, and married again, to a sweet and very wealthy man who doted on her and the children. If I were Kristal, I'd be sending Maggie bunches of flowers in gratitude.

'Maggie and I were so in love,' Dominic added pitifully. 'I just don't understand what happened.'

It's addictive, that in-love stuff. But *it doesn't last.*

Marriage, unlike an affair, has an ebb and flow. The swoon factor isn't 10 out of 10 all the time. Sometimes it will be, of course; you'll have moments when you feel exactly the way you did the first day you set eyes on each other. Others, you'll be irritated just by having to be in the same room. There are peaks and troughs, good days and bad; if you can average 6 or 7 out of 10, you're doing pretty well.

But some people begin to panic when that addictive, dizzying swoon sensation starts to fade. They confuse being 'in love' with the steady, infinitely less exciting but infinitely more enduring, married love. Desperate to recapture that lost feeling, they start searching for someone who can give it to them.

A man who's been married four times usually isn't a Philanderer, as people assume. He's an incurable romantic. Which is a thousand times worse.

If your man is caught up in the thrill of a love affair, you've got your work cut out to bring him back down to earth. But don't lose heart. There's an awful lot of schmaltz and myth surrounding the whole 'in love' thing, but at the end of the day it's just about chemistry. She isn't his bloody soulmate. (OK, I hate to tell you this, but there's no such thing. And that's *good*, because with six-billion-plus people stuck on this planet, finding The One, your destined other, would be like searching for a needle in a haystack of needles. I'm all for widening the pool a little.)

Falling 'in love' with another woman is no better or worse than an affair based on lots of bouncy sex. Just chemistry, remember. He *will* grow out of it. It's no reflection on you, it doesn't mean you can't love each other again, and it's *not your fault*.

So don't throw in the towel just yet.

Because now we're going to beat the Bitch.

In a nutshell

Men who cheat are pathetic lying bastards . . . but not all affairs are equal

1. Accidental Adultery: men are weak, pathetic fools. Sometimes they have affairs by mistake, even when they love you

2. One Night Stands: sometimes they're just addicted to the thrill of the chase

3. Philanderers: they like women the way a cat likes a mouse. They will not change

4. Love Affairs: the worst kind. But it's just chemistry, remember

Chapter Eight
What Not to Do

As Hippocrates said (though not in his famous Oath; a common misconception), 'First, do no harm'.

This is a tough rule to abide by when you've just found out your husband is bedding another woman. You want to do quite a *bit* of harm, actually, to the pair of them.

The Bobbitt instinct runs deep. Frankly, for several years after our divorce, if I'd run across my husband and he was on fire, I'd have toasted marshmallows.

But there's a lot to be said for holding your fire and keeping your powder dry. (Strange, isn't it, how many metaphors to do with love and marriage are military in tone?)

Firstly, by taking a deep breath and counting to ten, to the power of ten, and then repeating approximately one thousand times or until homicidal tendencies abate, you're giving yourself a chance to get over that first insane, unthinking, emotional response – which may be the opposite of what, deep down, you *really* want to do.

You may *think* you want out of the marriage; you may be quite certain you want nothing more to do with the lying, cheating son of a bitch. You believe throwing him out will somehow help you take back control, get over the betrayal and ameliorate the pain; but it frequently does nothing of the sort. It's not leaving (or, indeed, staying) that heals you, but understanding – and coming to terms with – what caused the affair in the first place.

On the other hand, you may believe you want to hang on to your marriage at all costs. The very idea of divorce, of becoming a single parent and having to cope alone, scares you shitless. If that's your reason for staying with him, trust me, (a) it's no guarantee *he* won't leave *you*; and (b) even if he doesn't, you're going to spend the rest of your life bloody miserable.

You need to get beyond this first, knee-(the)-jerk reaction. Letting your feelings settle for a brief period of time before you do anything helps you sift what you *really* feel from what you think you *should* feel; often without you even being aware of the process.

I'm not recommending the turn-a-blind-eye celebrity-wife approach, unless you've chosen, with eyes-wide-shut malice aforethought, to accept he'll never be faithful; a tough option only for those hopelessly married to a Philanderer. Many women would argue that this approach means you become part of the affair; you enable it. All true, but so what? This is *your* marriage, remember. Do what's right for you, and to hell with what anyone else thinks.

You *will* need to talk to him, but on your own terms, when you're emotionally and practically prepared.

This temporary time-out isn't about denial, or burying your head in the sand. It's about regrouping: giving yourself time to absorb the shock, so that when you do act, it's from a position of strength.

Confronting him too early can backfire spectacularly.
First, unless you have hard evidence, preferably glossy
10x8s of the two of them At It, he'll deny everything. You'll
walk away from the encounter convinced you're a paranoid,
suspicious cow.

Second, confrontation is exactly what the Bitch wants.
It's why she leaves her knickers in the glove compartment of
his car, or slips her lipstick into the pocket of his coat. It's
the reason she makes anonymous phone calls to your home,
or in some instances storms round to your house to tell all.

She wants to force the issue between you, and have you
throw him out. For where else will he have to turn but to
her?

Don't play into her hands. If and when you confront your
husband, it should be *your* decision, not hers.

Even if you do have the proof to force him into an admission, you'll naturally be emotional, unable to think clearly,
wounded beyond imagining and functioning on auto-pilot.
He, meanwhile, will have had quite a bit longer to roll the
taste of divorce around his mouth. None of this is a shock
to *him*, apart from the fact that you now know, of course.
Don't tip your hand to him until you've regained the higher
ground.

You're not doing nothing. You're simply biding your
time.

The golden fleece

Keeping your mouth shut and the knife in the drawer has a
number of very real benefits, aside from allowing you to
take your showers alone if you so wish for the next twenty-

'Greg and I had been married about nine years when I noticed he'd started talking about my best friend, Liv, more than I did. He always seemed to know what she was up to on any given weekend, and when she came over to see me, the two of them spent more time chatting together in the kitchen than I did.

'I wanted to ignore the signs, but I just knew. I thought I could wait him out, but one night, it all came to a head – we'd both been drinking, and before I knew it, I was screaming my head off at him. He broke down and admitted it. He said he didn't want a divorce, but he refused to stop seeing her.

'I lost it. I yelled and swore at him, and threatened to take the kids and the house and leave him with nothing. I raked up every little argument we'd ever had in the past – I called him a loser and a no-hoper, and said I despised him and always had. I told him he was the worst fuck I'd ever had, and Liv was only with him out of pity. I said everyone would laugh at him when they found out: she was the village bike, and was only after him for his money.

'It went on and on and on for hours. I felt like I was in some kind of soap opera; I was almost high on the drama.

'Eventually, Greg marched upstairs and packed a suitcase. I wanted to stop him leaving, but my pride wouldn't let me.

'His affair with Liv fizzled out almost immediately, and Greg and I went to counselling and tried again. But we couldn't get past that terrible fight. The things we said to each other couldn't be unsaid. In the end, we both agreed we had no choice but to split up. I wish with all my heart I could take back that night. I think we'd still be together if I hadn't said those awful things.'

Allison, 38, hair stylist

five to life. It gives you a chance to get your financial and practical safety net in place.

It's hard when your heart is breaking to think about money, but trust me, not having any isn't going to mend it. If he leaves you for the Bitch, you're going to have the fight of your life to keep your head above water.

Forget the myth that women walk away with the house, the kids and his pension, and the poor, fleeced husband ends up in a draughty bedsit drinking Cup-a-Soup.

Those idiots who scale Buckingham Palace with placards and whine about being broke and not getting enough access to their kids should be thrown in the Tower of London. Half – yes, *50 per cent* – of men lose touch with their own children within a year of divorce or separation *by choice*. Can you imagine the hue and cry if mothers did this?

Women get screwed post-divorce, mainly because children live with them. It's what you want, of course (unless the little fuckers are teenagers) but there's no getting away from the fact that it frequently messes up your chances of a lucrative, fast-track career. Or any kind of sex life, come to that.

He still has the income, and what maintenance he pays – *if* he pays it; many squirm off the hook – is considerably less than he was shelling out when he was both supporting the family and keeping the Bitch in Agent Provocateur.

You, meanwhile, are either still at home looking after the children, or working and juggling pay-through-the-nose childcare. You can't live off his maintenance; but when you try to supplement it, every penny you earn reduces the amount he pays you. You're in a lose-lose situation.

For these reasons, on average, a man's disposable income

rises immediately and continuously after a divorce, by an average of 25 per cent, whereas a woman's *falls* by a fifth. According to the Institute for Social and Economic Research, separated women have a poverty rate *three times* that of their former husbands.

So if you split up, you really need a good divorce. And 90 per cent of this comes down to doing your homework.

This strange, dreadful limbo you're in right now is also a golden opportunity, one of those rare times when you've got the jump on him. You've been forewarned. You know what he's up to, but *he* doesn't yet know you know. Take the time to get your financial ducks in a row and be ready if and when the moment comes – I'll explain how in detail in Chapter Twelve: Don't Get Mad, Get Diamonds.

Finally, and perhaps most importantly, this time in the calm before the storm gives you the chance to fuck up his cosy little affair once and for all, and totally change the outcome.

The slapper's tale (part II)

Please don't think I don't know what I'm asking of you when I tell you to wait. I know just how hard it is; and *precisely* how much it hurts.

I discovered my husband's affair seven years after we met, when we were on holiday with our two sons, then three years old and ten months. I'd taken the children down to the hotel pool while he finished a few business calls upstairs, but when I unpacked my beach bag, I realized I'd only packed the kids' factor nine million, and not my own fry-you-to-a-crisp skin-cancer oil. So I left the children with a friend, and ran back upstairs to get it.

I'd forgotten my sunscreen, that's all. Odd how one simple oversight can change your life.

As I opened the bedroom door, I heard him talking into his phone out on the balcony. Assuming it was work, I tiptoed in so as not to disturb him. And stepped off a cliff.

There was no question of my making a mistake, or jumping to conclusions. His end of the conversation left no room for doubt. He was having an affair.

My first instinct was to howl with pain and grief and fury and fly out there to confront him (or possibly push him off the balcony), but somehow I held back. Instinctively, I knew that for the boys' sake (and to avoid the trifling inconvenience of a murder charge) I had to keep a clear head and think everything through first. I needed to keep my wits about me if I wanted to save my marriage; even more so if it turned out we were headed for the divorce courts.

Somehow I got through the rest of our holiday without giving the game away, putting my withdrawn listlessness and sudden fits of uncontrollable tears down to a 'nasty bug'. (A real Bitch of a one, in fact.) As soon as we got home, I turned our house upside-down looking for . . . for *what* I didn't quite know, but I was certain I'd recognize it when I found it.

It didn't take long. There, in black and white on our phone bill, was the number he'd called every day, often three or four times (no wonder the bill was in triple digits), for the previous six months.

With a little more digging, I soon discovered who she was, where she lived, when and how they'd met; in fact, more than I could ever have wanted to know about every gut-wrenching, soul-destroying aspect of their affair.

Adultery is so much more than the breaking of a promise. It destroys not only your present and your future, but also your past. It undermines all you thought you knew and could count on. You question everything. You trust no one. You replay every moment of your shared history, combing it for false notes, hints, clues, *something* you missed. You can't believe in anything any more. All the good times, the precious memories, are suddenly tainted: your first kiss, the moment he proposed, your wedding night, the birth of each of your children; every Christmas, every holiday, every touch. *When did our lives stop being real? When was the smile first faked? When did the promise of love become a lie?*

Dirty knickers

I air my unsavoury smalls in public not to pillory my ex-husband again (we've caused each other enough pain and misery to last a lifetime) but to explain that (a) *I get it*: yes, I *do* know how much this is killing you; and (b) there is a right way and a wrong way to handle what happens next. And unfortunately, like so many women, I picked Option Two.

(Oh, all right. Maybe I want to pillory him a *tiny* bit. I admit it: in many ways, I neglected him shamefully. But as I've said, sleeping with someone else doesn't exactly *help*, does it?)

I found out about my husband's infidelity in a savagely

swift and shocking way; I wouldn't wish it on my worst (well, maybe my *worst* . . . you know who you are) enemy. But in retrospect, of course, all the signs he was having an affair had actually been there for months. If only I'd had that nifty little Bobbitt Quiz to hand.

A sudden fancy for black Levi's, when previously I hadn't been able to prize him out of his Gap khakis and into jeans of *any* colour for love nor money. A new passion for re-arranging our basement storage room at all hours of the day and night. The discovery that his mobile strangely no longer worked from home; he always had to walk 200 yards up our road to the top of a hill to have a conversation on it. (Clearly a crucial satellite had been shot down from space while I wasn't looking.) He suddenly couldn't stand to be around my parents, with whom he'd always got on well before. Ditto my friends. And, in fact, *me*.

I could bore (and, indeed, have bored) for hours on the subject of How Stupid *Was* I? I shall, however, on this occasion be mercifully brief. Let's just say that he pretty much ticked every red alert box. I *should* have known. Perhaps if I hadn't just had a baby, I might have noticed more. Perhaps it was my *lack* of notice that was part of the problem.

In the immediate aftermath of the discovery, I took grim consolation in the fact that although the affair had been going on for some time, he still hadn't actually walked out yet. If he doesn't leave in the first six months, he probably won't (though *you* may choose to jettison *him*, of course).

But I didn't know what to do next, or where to turn for help. Embarrassed by what felt like my failure as a wife, as a *woman*, I couldn't tell anyone. I was emotionally frozen in place, a rabbit caught in the headlights. In the end, almost by default, I decided to play a waiting game; instead of confronting him, I prayed the affair would blow itself out.

So I smiled nicely when my husband told me he was popping out to 'pick up a newspaper', knowing he was really escaping to ring *her*. I washed and folded clothes I knew she'd see him remove.

I packed a suitcase she would unpack for him. Planned a Christmas together I didn't know if he'd be around to share.

The strain was intolerable. I lost weight (the adultery diet; I should write a book) and started to smoke, which I'd never done in my life. My husband had always travelled a great deal for work, but now, knowing that when he was away he was with *her*, I started going out more and more often in his absence, leaving the children with a babysitter and partying until dawn. Achingly miserable, I cried myself to sleep every night for months.

I struggled on like this for far too long: nearly a year. In that time, it became easier to bear: I didn't realize it then, but I was slowly severing the ties of our marriage one by one. I thought that in waiting him out I was doing nothing, but in fact I was unconsciously putting more distance between us every day. I did my grieving and raging and healing before we'd even gone our separate ways.

Our marriage died without either of us even noticing.

Elephants on parade

In many ways, as I've said, my approach was the right one. Confronting him before you've got your shit together emotionally and practically can be disastrous. But you can't lose sight of your goal: Beating the Bitch. You're supposed to be *waiting*, not paralysed.

I was certain I wanted to save my marriage; I had two very young children, I believed in marriage, and I loved my husband. I chose to hold fire, telling myself that if I was patient this silly fling would blow over, and our marriage would emerge stronger than ever. Yet my withdrawal from any kind of marital engagement (see, that military stuff again) told a different story.

I waited too long. I had a chance to turn things around, and I stepped back from it. So perhaps I didn't really want to fix it as much as I thought I did.

Partly it was because I'm crap at confrontation. I'm a strong, independent, high-maintenance woman (ask either of my husbands – it's the one thing they can agree on), and yet the truth is I run gibbering with terror from any kind of face-to-face conflict. I have absolutely no idea why, but it may have something to do with my parents' loud, happy, forthright, confrontational forty-year marriage. Or my good-girl teacher's-pet desire to please everyone. Or perhaps I'm just a bloody wuss.

And partly I think I wanted things to blow up in my face. I'd never have admitted it to myself at the time, but I wasn't happy either. I let my marriage die *because I wanted to*.

Of course I shouldn't have sat on my hands for more than a year without saying anything. (In the opinion of most of my friends, I should have put them round the bugger's neck and squeezed.)

My predecessor had raged and smacked my husband (sorry, *her* husband) until he ran off with me just to get some peace and quiet. I dealt with the problem by shutting him out altogether. I didn't talk to him, other than to discuss parking tickets or the mortgage; how could I, given the elephant in the room? Neither of us wanted to get down and dirty and actually *discuss* our relationship: he didn't want to give himself away and, frankly, I couldn't bear to listen to him lie.

We rarely had sex; when we did, it was rough and angry. We didn't go out for a meal or a movie: I couldn't stand to be alone with him. I couldn't stand *him*, really.

So I pulled up the drawbridge, dropped the portcullis and waited for him to storm the battlements with protestations of love and remorse. Naturally enough, he ran off with my successor. Neither my approach, nor that of the previous incumbent, was what you might call a raging success.

Dance away

The harsh truth of the matter is that I drove him into her bed. I might as well have laid out her lingerie and turned back the covers. How could I hope to Beat the Bitch by treating the man as if he was a leper with bird flu? Hmm. On the one hand, a willing and pliant girl who treats him with awe and respect and goes down on him nightly. On the other, a frigid cow who glares at him for daring to open his eyes in the morning and fingers the paring knife lovingly when he wanders into the kitchen in his boxers.

You might as well call it 'constructive divorce'. Such was the Arctic wind whistling down our bed at night, I practically invited him to climb into a warmer one.

No, of course I'm not *defending* him. I'm simply telling it like it is, girls. You may *know* he's in the wrong, but how warm will your self-righteousness keep you? Are you in this to win it, or are you happy to rest on your moral laurels?

Two years after we separated, when the dust had finally settled, my husband and I had a frank and forthright discussion about our marriage in a way we had never done while we were still in it.

'I didn't want to get divorced again,' he admitted, 'but you were such a *bitch*. If you had been a bit nicer to me, and thought about what I wanted for once, I wouldn't have looked elsewhere.'

I pointed out, tactfully, that if he hadn't looked elsewhere I wouldn't have been such a bitch.

'Be fair,' he protested. 'I would never have left you if you hadn't had an affair too!'

We don't need to go into that last bit now— Oh, we do? Can't I just . . . all right, all right. In the interests of science, and so that you can Learn From My Mistakes, next on my list of What *Not* to Do is: have a retaliatory affair.

Or, in my case (ever one to over-egg the pudding), two.

The goose's sauce

The first happened about six months after I discovered my husband's shiny new secret life.

The worst part about his affair, after the initial shock and pain had passed, had been the *loneliness*. For years, my husband had been my best friend, the person I turned to first with exciting news, a funny anecdote, a problem, an idea; and he had done the same with me. But not any more. Now, *she* was the one whose shoulder he cried on, and whose dreams and hopes he shared.

Loneliness, crooned Bryan Ferry, is a crowded room. An unhappy marriage can be the loneliest place of all.

It's not just the emotional isolation, though, is it? It's a *physical* thing too. Not so much the sex – although there's nothing like not getting it to make you miss it – but the ordinary, everyday physical contact: the kisses, the hugs, the arm round your shoulders, the squeeze of a hand. Children are wonderful at giving all of these things, of course, but it's not the same. I missed it desperately. I missed my husband, *I missed a man*. I felt like I had a glass wall around me that nothing and no one could breach.

Having your husband turn from you to another woman – especially a younger woman – is so *insulting*. Of course you want to see that spark in a man's eye again. You want to feel sexy, desirable, *wanted*, instead of like an old shoe (and a Birkenstock at that).

And yes, you want to get your own back. Why not? You want to taste some of that goose's sauce. For all of these reasons, and probably a good few more, an affair of your own can seem like a bloody good idea.

It isn't.

My first fling was a one-night stand with a friend of my husband's. There had always been a *frisson* between us, and it didn't take much – some salsa music and a few caipirinhas, in fact – to fan the spark into a . . . well, into another spark, actually.

He was hot. Young. *Energetic*. But he wasn't my husband, and instead of feeling triumphant and empowered, I scrambled off his futon (yes, it was that sort of fling) feeling cheap, dirty and even more miserable, if that were possible.

Falling into bed with someone else was bad enough. But then, three months later, I went and fancied myself in love. And that was infinitely worse.

I was in no condition to do something as risky as fall in love. Frankly, I wouldn't have trusted me to fall in a six-inch puddle safely. Emotionally, I was all over the map. Wary and clingy, over-enthusiastic and suspicious, distant and suffocating. I hadn't even begun to heal. I couldn't begin to cope.

The relationship was doomed from the start. When it ended, as it inevitably did, it hurt even more, if that were possible, than the break-up of my marriage; in large part because the failure was cumulative. But worse than that, it distracted me at the most crucial time in my life. I was so wrapped up in this new, passionate, exciting romance that I stopped caring about the old, painful, messy one. I *could* perhaps have saved my marriage. The conversation we had after we separated showed me that. But I lost my focus at the critical point, and suddenly it was too late.

Don't. Just . . . don't

One last and unequivocal no-no, before we move on to what you *should* be doing in the next chapter.

Don't. Get. Pregnant.

I'm not going to say any more on this one. If you can't see it, I can't help you.

Don't give up

Bel Mooney is a respected writer and broadcaster, the author of numerous books for adults and children, and presenter of many programmes for TV and BBC Radio 4. She now writes a weekly column for the Saturday edition of the Daily Mail, *advising readers on emotional and relationship issues.*

She was married to television journalist Jonathan Dimbleby for thirty-five years, until the couple separated in 2004 after his affair with an opera singer. They have two adult children. In 2007 she married Robin Allison-Smith, a freelance photographer.

'I am convinced that couples can survive an affair. I don't say it's easy; it's never easy, but plenty of people manage it, and the rather crude suggestion of "Show the bastard the door" is pub advice. Although an affair can be very, very destructive, it should be the cue to do some work on the marriage, not just ditch everything with no effort.

'When there are children involved I think it's absolutely incumbent on a couple to make every effort to save their marriage, and not just fall at the first hurdle. But there's no point trying to save the relationship if you can't forgive him. You'll never forget, you'll never ever forget, but it is possible to forgive. How? I can't tell someone how to forgive, it's a very individual, personal thing. But this is the kind of suggestion I make: to somehow put yourself in the other person's position, look in the mirror, and realize that there are things within the relationship that need talking through. If you can ask yourself if there was any way at all that you contributed to what happened, it is possible to work towards a state of forgiveness.

'Effectively, you have to say, "This happened, you're sorry for it, I'm sorry for it, let's work on our relationship and go forward."

'This is predicated on an infidelity which is a blip, not a life-changing affair, when a marriage breaks up because someone has fallen deeply in love. That's a different kettle of fish: it's bloody and it's awful, and there's blood all over the floor for the person who's hurt. In the end, you have to be philosophical – I'm a great believer in Fate – and tell yourself the marriage simply wasn't meant to be. Some marriages run their course . . . and in the end both parties are liberated.

'I view life in endless nuances of grey. I don't see things as black and white. Human beings are incredibly complicated. I look at all the books in my library . . . all the poems and all the prose that's been written about pain, the endless ways in which people hurt each other, and how they somehow come through it and go on surviving. That's rather how I see marriage – as a source of potential pain and potential joy. It's the most demanding test of character most of us ever face.

'The key to moving forward is to accept that things are going to be different from now on. Counselling is very important – hugely important. The truth about your feelings towards each other, and towards your marriage, must come out. And then you have to look at each other and say, "We're not the same people any more. We're different people. Can we make this work?"

'Imagine a priceless Ming vase in a museum. It gets dropped, and broken. A team of expert restorers put it back together, and it takes its place in the museum again, and to most observers it looks exactly the same; they could never tell it was smashed. But it was. It's different now; damaged.

> 'You must accept that your marriage has changed for ever. Then it can work – as a new structure. An affair is never a good thing, but perhaps, at the end of the day, some good can come out of it. You can end up with a truer marriage.'

We've just discussed what you *shouldn't* do. Now let's shoot for the bullseye: things you *should* do.

Keep reading.

In a nutshell

First do no harm

1. Don't confront him until you've got your shit together
2. Don't yell, call him names, tell him he sucks in bed, or refer to his penis as a pathetic shrivelled piece of limp spaghetti (well, not out loud)
3. Protect yourself financially. Knowledge is power, remember
4. Bide your time . . . but don't die of old age waiting for the right moment
5. Don't go for constructive divorce. Give him a reason to stay
6. Don't have a retaliatory affair (and definitely not two)
7. Don't get pregnant
8. Don't give up

Chapter Nine
Beat the Bitch!

I've said it before (and fully intend to again, just as soon as they make the movie of my life): men are simple creatures. Their needs are few.

Affection. Approval. Sex. And not necessarily in that order.

They're easily led astray – the poor mindless ninnies – but on the plus side, it isn't hard to round them up and bring them home again. By and large, they really *don't* want to leave you.

You just need a plan. And as luck would have it . . .

Here's one I made earlier

What's required is a three-pronged attack, rather like the points of the pitchfork you'd happily drive into the Bitch's heart. (Or am I thinking of vampires? So easy to get your lethal blood-sucking parasitic leeches muddled up.)

The first prong, as it were, is all about you.

The second is about him.

And the third, of course, is all about *her*.

Before we get down to brass . . . er, prongs, let me briefly address those cat-calling from the I-don't-believe-in-playing-games peanut gallery. You know who you are.

When a celebrity footballer or TV chef gets caught with his pants down, every columnist with an inch of print to spare pitches in with pithy advice. 'Dump him, dear.' 'Go for his millions.' 'A man who cheats with you will cheat on you.'

Celebrity wives who've already trodden this path write 'open letters' in the tabloids. Morning chat shows hold phone-ins on whether the love rat in question should be given a second chance (0.1 per cent), or shown the red card (99.9 per cent).

Minus a cheque with lots of zeros from the red-tops for sharing our pain, it's not so different for the rest of us. Everyone you've ever met, from the postman to the girl who does your bikini wax, will chip in with their two penn'orth.

Your friends always thought he was a tosser (though they were happy enough to let him pay for dinner when you all went out). Your mother never liked him; she always said so, didn't she? (Actually, no; she thought he was Mr bloody Wonderful when he finally took you off her hands about five minutes before your ovaries expired.) Your sister reckons you're well rid: did she ever tell you about the time he put his hand on her bum when he was helping her do the Christmas washing-up? Even the damn cat hisses when he walks into the room.

'Dump him,' they chorus indignantly. 'How can you ever trust him again? You don't want to be one of those sad, undignified women who has to *play games* to keep him, do you?'

Leaving aside for the moment the fact that it's very easy to take the moral high ground when you're looking over the fence into someone else's garden, they're fundamentally *wrong*.

We *all* play games of one sort or another to help our relationships along. We tell little white lies; we laugh at our boss's crappy jokes; we assure our girlfriends those jeans make their bums look *fantastic*; we tell our mothers we love the audio tapes of the new papal biography they got us for Christmas.

Men and women alike manipulate, manoeuvre and hustle to get what they want – at work, in bed, and out of it.

When was the last time you bought a house and told the seller right off the bat the full amount you were prepared to pay? Or sold a home, and admitted to your buyer that his was the only sniff of interest you'd had in ten months, and that you'd cut a hundred thou off the asking price and throw in your first-born just to get the millstone off your neck?

A man knows exactly what he's doing when he waits three days before he calls you. So do you when you hold out for five dates before you sleep with him.

It's how the human race oils the wheels. What the hell do you think happens at Westminster or in the White House? You think everyone calls a spade a spade, or puts all their cards on the table face-up? Diplomacy, negotiating, compromising, call it what you will, it amounts to the same thing. People play games to achieve their own ends.

Not you? *Really?* When you were dating, I bet you shaved your legs and made sure your bra and knickers always matched, and don't tell me you went down on him in the car on the way back from meeting his parents because his mother's collection of Royal Doulton turned you on.

Too many women make the mistake of thinking marriage signals the end of 'having to play games'. As if not making the effort to seduce and allure is somehow a good thing.

The truth is that many women try far harder to impress their friends, their boss, their neighbours or a total bloody stranger than they do the man who's supposed to be the love of their life. His needs get shoved to the bottom of the pile, somewhere beneath feeding the guinea pig and doing the ironing, because we've all 'got too much on our plate'.

'I always feel like my needs and feelings come last. The kids are finally old enough to be fairly independent, and still my wife is too busy for me. She's always rushing off to yoga or the PTA or her book club. She loves having friends over – practically every weekend we have people round. She knows I'm tired and stressed at work, but when I ask her if we could just have one weekend to ourselves, she makes a big song and dance about how I'm ruining her social life, and if it was up to me we'd never see anyone.

'When we do go out by ourselves, she never makes any effort to get dressed up. She says there's no point putting on make-up, it's just going to come off again in a couple of hours. She has zero interest in sex. I want to be wanted – is that so hard to understand? When she can't be bothered to take the trouble to get dressed up, it's like she's saying I'm not worth it. She complains I'm not romantic, but she's the one who dropped the ball first. She'll make more effort to take the dog for a walk than she does for me.'

Anthony, 44, press officer

We expect a man to be understanding when we're hormonal, understanding when we don't feel like sex, understanding when we're stressed and frantic. But what about understanding *him*? What about *his* needs?

Men aren't complicated. They want to be admired, respected and appreciated; they want to know they're loved, and that they make us happy – not by doing things *for* us, or giving things *to* us, but simply by being who they are.

You picked him. You married him. Approval and love shouldn't require a huge leap of faith. And if showing it is 'playing games', I'm sorry but that's *exactly* what you should bloody well be doing.

It's much easier, of course, if he hasn't just climbed out of bed with the village bike. Happier for all concerned if it had never come to this (and for those of you lucky enough not to be an unwilling member of the Adultery Club – yet – go directly to Chapter Sixteen: You Don't Want to Hear This, But . . . You can thank me later).

Of course, if you still think that using your brain and boxing clever to win back your husband is undignified and beneath you, fine. Go cast a spell instead.

Spell to return lost love to you

This was given to me years ago by a rather fey friend (the kind my mother used to refer to as a 'dippy tart'). She insists it works. But I wouldn't recommend it. No, honestly, I *really* wouldn't. You know what they say: be careful what you wish for . . .

13 sacred steps to regain his love

If you really wish to proceed, entirely at your own risk, you will need:

- Altar or sacred space
- Red candle
- Salt
- Nail or knife
- Olive oil
- Red rose (with thorns)
- Matches
- 5–6 inch circle of red fabric
- Dried lavender
- Ylang-ylang oil
- Small piece of rose quartz
- Small piece of copper (a coin, ring or piece of wire is fine)
- Orange oil
- Small plate
- Blue ribbon

1. After collecting the tools and ingredients, prepare your space by lightly sprinkling salt in a circle around yourself while speaking the following words:

    I consecrate this place
    For the goddess within and without
    Only love and good can remain
    Hate and evil are cast out.

2. Carve his name on to the red candle. Do this lengthwise, with the use of a nail or knife, but be sure to stop carving an inch from the candle base.
3. Sprinkle olive oil on to your candle and place it in its holder.
4. Next, pluck seven thorns off the red rose. Stick these thorns into the letters of his name.

5. Light the candle and picture him falling in love with you again. Focus on this thought and think of nothing else. Then repeat this spell three times:

> *Powers of the universe*
> *Bring [his name] back to me.*
> *This is my will*
> *So mote it be.*

As your candle burns down to each thorn, he'll remember everything lovable about you and as a result will want to be with you, and only you, again.

6. Place the plate on the altar and set the red fabric circle on it. Take a pinch of the dried lavender and hold it in your clasped hands. Inhale the aroma of the lavender while repeating the same incantation three times.
7. Rubbing your hands together, allow the lavender to sprinkle on to the red fabric circle.
8. Place a few drops of the ylang-ylang oil on to your hands and then begin to rub the oil into the piece of quartz, again saying the spell three times.
9. Place the piece of rose quartz on to the red fabric.
10. Place a few drops of the orange oil onto your hands and rub the oil into the piece of copper while saying the incantation three times.
11. Place the piece of copper on to the red fabric.
12. Take the red candle and hold it above the fabric. Allow one drop of wax to fall on to each of the items gathered below.
13. Gather up the circle to form a pouch. Use the blue ribbon to close it tightly with seven knots. Bury the pouch beneath an oak, rowan or holly tree, and wait for your spell to accomplish its goal.

(Yes, I did actually try this once, in a moment of Chablis-induced nothing-to-lose desperation after I'd been dumped by the crush of my life.

It all went swimmingly until I tried to bury the sacred pouch beneath a tree. I was living in a tiny flat in London at the time, and the only tree within a mile radius was in someone else's front garden.

I had to steal out to do the deed under cover of darkness, and as I scrabbled madly, guiltily looking over my shoulder all the while, I managed to exhume the partially decomposed remains of my neighbour's pet cat. A truly delightful experience. Not.

On the plus side, however, the man in question rang three days later, told me he'd changed his mind and declared his undying love.

We gave it another go, but frankly the whole dead-cat thing cast rather a pall. I broke up with him after a week, and spent the next six months screening his increasingly psychotic phone calls. Like I said, be careful what you wish for.)

It's all about you

Unless you're really a fan of dancing in the moonlight and partially decomposed household pets, you might want to stick with Plan A.

The first thing we need to take care of is *you*: your health and well-being. You've got an extraordinary fight ahead of you, and at the moment, punch-drunk and reeling with misery, you probably couldn't take on a disabled goldfish and win.

If you seriously want to beat the Bitch, you need to look after yourself before you do anything. This sounds obvious, but when you're as wounded as you are right now, it's easily pushed on to the back burner. You're in a really bad place: disorientated, bewildered, depressed and sick to your stomach. The thought of getting out of bed and facing the world is quite simply overwhelming. One part of you wants to curl up under the duvet and never get dressed again. The other part wants to go out and get steamingly drunk.

Your mental state can be summed up in four words: *What is the point?*

It's hard to get excited by anything right now. Your job, your home, your appearance – none of it seems to matter much any more.

Unfortunately, this mental, emotional and often physical collapse is happening right when you need all your resources as never before. It's not all over; what you do – or *don't* do, as we discussed in the previous chapter – next *does* matter, more than you can possibly imagine right now.

You need to be at the top of your game. You've got everything to play for. You have to recover your wits and your energy p.d.q.

Three things will do this for you, and at the risk of sounding like your mother (if she's anything like mine, she's right more often than anyone else on earth) they are: exercising, eating well, and somehow finding a way to relax and be happy, if only in the small things.

Remember, this is a *crisis*! You need to look after yourself properly to avoid getting sick and run-down. You can't fight the Bitch with one arm tied behind your back. (And a snotty red nose isn't a good look for anyone, never mind a wife trying to reclaim her errant husband.)

Kick-box clever

Exercising is probably the last thing you feel like doing right now, but (oh help, now I sound like the Green Goddess) pulling the covers over your head isn't the answer. It'll just make you feel even more listless and depressed, and probably give you a permanent headache into the bargain.

Get up. Find your jogging bottoms and trainers, and get moving. Don't wait to 'feel like it' – it'll never happen. It doesn't really matter what you do, though I'd recommend classes (step, pump, salsa) over anything solitary. Working out in the weights room is too boring and too lonely unless you're hyper-motivated (or the instructor looks like Daniel Craig) and jogging has never done it for me: my boobs bounce too much, there's too much dog shit on the pavements, and anyway, the slightest cloud is enough for me to wimp out.

Thumping the shit out of a punchbag while imagining the Bitch's face pasted onto it will, by contrast, make you feel one hell of a lot better about life. (For this reason, kick-boxing is a personal favourite of mine.)

You'll also release all those much-hyped endorphins, which will give you a natural high almost as effective as a large G&T. (You may think this is one of those myths put about by annoyingly perky gym mavens who get some sort of masochistic pleasure out of prancing around in leotards, but trust me, it's actually true.)

And you'll finally shift that last ten pounds of baby weight, and emerge like a butterfly from your cellulite chrysalis. It's amazing how good getting into your skinny pre-kids jeans will make you feel.

In bed with Boris

Hand in hand with exercising goes eating properly. Women in distress go one of two ways, and you already know which you are. Some of us lose our appetites and shrink two dress sizes in as many weeks – you may think this is a good thing, but (a) losing weight fast just makes your face fall in on itself so you end up looking like a Hollywood celebrity but without the bank balance; and (b) men don't like skinny women. *Really.* They don't.

Alternatively, you'll stuff yourself with as many carbs, fats and sugars as you can cram into your body without your teeth falling out. This will leave you bloated, sluggish and lardy. Men don't like taking emaciated skeletons to bed, but they don't want to curl up with Boris Johnson either.

Don't punish your body because your husband couldn't keep his trousers zipped. You need all your reserves to fight the Bitch. Think of yourself as an athlete in training. You wouldn't run a marathon without tuning your body, or expect it to perform at its best on a carrot a day – or twenty-four Mars Bars. You can't take on the Bitch and win if you're not playing your A-game.

So be kind to yourself: don't lacerate yourself with guilt over every Flake or glass of Pinot, but don't pig out comfort eating and turn into a lard-arse either.

That takes care of the body. Now let's think about your soul. You need to relax; but remember (and I speak from desperate experience here): drinking, smoking and/or screwing around aren't the answer.

This is where your friends come in. Turn to them, but make it clear from the beginning that you need them to love you, support you, reassure you that you're not a minging troll and take you out of yourself; not to diss your man, give you advice or pass judgement.

Don't flail around pouring out your heart to every passing acquaintance. Be discreet. You know the girls you can really trust, the two or three friends who'd walk with you to the ends of the earth if you asked it.

Talk about what you're going through, but try not to build a case against him; the last thing you need is to back yourself into a corner where your pride forces you to make decisions, rather than your head or your heart.

Spoil yourself. Go to a spa – and I mean one of those places where they wrap you in warm towels and rub delicious-smelling unguents into your skin, not some sort of Nazi concentration camp where they feed you two peas and a limp piece of tofu before making you drop and give them twenty.

Up the retail therapy. A little shopping goes a long way, and incidentally, it's very good for boosting your alimony claims if the worst comes to the worst (we'll get to this in Chapter Twelve: Don't Get Mad, Get Diamonds).

Schadenfreude is a wonderful thing

Try looking out for someone who's even worse off than you. I'm not talking about your forty-something single girlfriend who can't find a man, is being deafened by her biological clock and has just been made redundant. (Though admittedly your life now looks positively blooming in comparison to hers. Schadenfreude is greatly underrated if you ask me.)

Not to get all Shakespearean on you, but altruism is twice blest: it blesseth him that gives, and him that takes.

Instead of sitting around weeping into your fourteenth doughnut of the day, go out and *do* something – help in a soup kitchen, raise funds for Cancer Research, join Meals on Wheels. Anything that makes you feel good about yourself. You can all too easily become consumed with your own problems; all that navel-gazing will give you a crick in your neck. Get your mind off yourself now and then, and you'll be surprised how much better you feel.

Finally, be aware that sometimes you *can't* just pull yourself together without professional help. Depression is frequently a physiological illness, *not* a mental one, caused by a lack of feel-good biochemicals in the brain. If you were diabetic, you'd take insulin; if you were anaemic, you'd pop a few iron supplements. *Depression is no different.*

If your body requires a chemical you can't supply right now, prescription medication may be what it *needs*. It's nothing to be ashamed of; you're not weak or a failure for requiring help. Usually, a brief period of taking anti-depressants will kick-start your body into producing the chemicals you need again, and you'll be able to go it alone before too long. Left untreated, however, depression can blight your life and those of the people who depend on you.

Symptoms can be dramatic, like constantly bursting into violent tears, or more subtle, like tiredness, insomnia, lack of focus, backaches and headaches. If they last longer than a few weeks, don't keep struggling on alone. *Get help*.

Flannelette pyjamas

By now, you should know the difference between an Accidental Affair, a One Night Stand, a Love Affair and a Philandering Fling.

(If you don't, you either have the attention span of a goldfish with ADHD – you're not a *man*, are you? – or you're standing in Tesco flicking through this book to see if it's worth shelling out for. Trust me, it is. Now buy the wretched thing, take it home, go back to Chapter Seven and catch up with the rest of us.)

If your man is Surbiton's answer to Don Juan, you're just going to have to suck it up, girlfriend. Learn to live with it; or stop the music, get off the ride, and go directly to Chapter Twelve: Don't Get Mad, Get Diamonds. He's doing it because he gets a kick out of the actual *cheating*. It has nothing to do with sex, or the extraordinary things the Bitch can do to a cherry stalk with her tongue. He likes the challenge, the chase, the *kill*.

I'm not saying it's *impossible* to stop a Philanderer looking elsewhere. If you're so proficient in the art of reinventing yourself that you make Madonna look bland and predictable; if you get off on drama and histrionics and almighty break-ups followed by divine make-ups; if you hate your husband as much as you love him and can really, deep-down-so-that-he-knows-you-mean-it threaten to walk out; in short, if you're Katharine Hepburn in *The Lion in*

Winter, then by all means knock yourself out. Challenge him; let him chase you. Do all the above and more. You may not keep him faithful, but you'll certainly keep him busy.

Most of us, however, are not shacked up with a Philanderer. We're stuck with a dolt who made a mistake, or a chap who's had his head turned by the office vamp (think Alan Rickman in *Love, Actually*), or a loser who needs some two-bit hussy hanging on his every word to feel good about himself.

Think hard about your louse – sorry, *spouse* – and precisely *why* he might be playing away. Be really honest with yourself. I know it's painful, but now is not the time for emotional breakdowns, girls. We need to be tough and clear-eyed about this, because you can bet your flannelette pyjamas *she* is.

If you want to beat the competition, you have to figure out what she's doing for him that you're not – and then do it better. That's not playing games: it's looking after your own.

There's a good reason he's getting jiggy with another woman – note: I said *reason*, not excuse – and if you're going to stop him, you'd damn well better find out what it is.

Marks on the carpet

Affairs aren't about sex. They're about a man not feeling valued, or respected, or the boss in his own home. They're about temptation, inadequacy and boredom; about feeling neglected or taken for granted. A man needs to be admired, approved of and appreciated. Right?

Er . . . nope. All the above is true, of course, but affairs *are* about sex. *Obviously.* Otherwise you wouldn't be getting your very sensible M&S knickers in a twist now, would you?

The single thing that differentiates his affair with the Bitch from his relationship with your best friend (unless they're one and the same) is that he's shagging the Bitch. And she's probably a lot more enthusiastic and inventive about the whole thing than you are.

I'm not trying to be mean. You've been climbing into bed with him for a lot longer than she has, and you've both got a bit lazy. You take short-cuts. A 'quickie' is the norm. You don't want to wake the kids/get marks on the carpet/pull the cupboard door off its hinges. You don't dress up in fishnets and suspenders, and I doubt he's bothering (with the male equivalent, I mean) either.

The problem is that when it comes to sex, we're all paddling upstream. There's no getting away from the fact that familiarity breeds boredom, if not contempt. Remember our four men in a bar at the start of this book, three of whom will cheat?

While they're sitting there trying to figure out which one of them is the loser who hasn't cheated, a beautiful woman walks through the door. A curtain of shimmering blond hair hangs to her waist. She's wearing a sexy scarlet dress that hugs her perfect curves and shows off tanned legs that come up to here. Conversation stops. Every male eye swivels in her direction. Then one of our quartet leans in and mutters to his friends: 'Somewhere, there's a man who's bored out of his mind making love to her.'

See? We're back to the old-pussy problem again.

Domesticity destroys sexual desire, no matter how loving a couple may be. Eroticism requires novelty, mystery and risk.

This dilemma isn't something you can solve. It's a paradox you *manage*.

Unlike love, sexual excitement doesn't play by the rules. It's politically incorrect, thriving on unfair advantages, the exertion of control, power games, passive-aggressive manipulation, seduction, withholding and subtle cruelties.

When we settle into a long-term relationship, we put all this crap aside, assuming we shouldn't need to play games anymore. But the fundamental nature of desire doesn't change.

When was the last time you tried something new? Does the thought of having him drizzle champagne on your naked body turn you on, or make you sigh inwardly at the thought of changing the sheets midweek?

Do you own any sex aids, apart from a vibrator (come on, that's hardly ground-breaking: we've all had one since *Cosmo* told us to Own Our Orgasms back in the Eighties)? Anal beads? Nipple clamps? A pair of handcuffs?

You think it's all a bit embarrassing, right? A bit sleazy, or cheesy, or sad? An anal probe and some KY jelly may not do it for you – they may not do it for him either – but this isn't about *you*. Women are so busy ensuring their right to climax in bed isn't compromised, we've all but forgotten about him.

Men are visual creatures. They *like* all that Playboy stuff. Peekaboo sheer camisoles, seamed stockings, schoolgirl braids and a short pleated gym skirt.

They like novelty. You may be old pussy, but with a bit of

imagination and effort, you can *seem* like new pussy time and again.

'When my wife is out of town, it's just me and my right hand. I wank every night. Why not? It feels great, plus I sleep better and it's a great stress-buster.

'If it were up to me, I'd jerk off every day of my life. But my wife would freak out. She'd take it personally. I want to say to her, "You don't want to have sex with me every night – you're too tired or not in the mood – so what's the harm?"

'But no. I can't have sex with her, and I can't wank without her. I wish someone would print a headline in those women's magazines: "Let Your Man Wank and Save Your Marriage!"'

Eric, 35, office manager

You don't have to turn into a hooker to keep him hooked. I'm not suggesting you rush into Ann Summers and panic-buy. But if you want to Beat the Bitch in the bedroom for good, there are three Golden Rules:

1. Have sex a lot more often; *never* turn him down.
2. Initiate sex – nothing will turn him on more than thinking you want him.
3. Make sex more interesting, more of an adventure, and more unpredictable. (If you're short of ideas, check out the next chapter. Or buy one of my saucy novels.)

Intimacy shmintimacy!

I hate to be the one to tell you, girls, but on this one men have got it right. Intimacy *is* something to fear.

The common mantra is that the solution to the conflict between love and desire is increased closeness. Intimacy, intimacy, intimacy! If we talk more, share more, communicate more, it will lead to better sex.

But in fact just the *opposite* is true.

> 'It's not the lack of intimacy that inhibits desire, but too much. In our love life we want closeness, but desire needs space. There's nothing wrong with living in close proximity, but it doesn't bode well for eroticism. Our partner becomes known and fraternal, and sex needs the unknown, the risky, to thrive.
>
> 'If you have too much distance, of course you suffer from a lack of connection, but merging, on the other hand, kills desire. In order to have a spark, there needs to be a gap, but if there is too big a gap, the spark cannot cross.'
>
> **Esther Perel, *Mating in Captivity: Reconciling the Erotic and the Domestic***

The spark doesn't come naturally. You have to be wilful and intentional about desire. If you wait for the right moment, it'll never come. You have to *make* it happen.

Premeditate. Build anticipation. Don't rely on spontaneity – we all associate being spontaneous with the start of a relationship, when it's all new and exciting, but in fact we're more calculating during this period than at any other time. Women dress in sexy lingerie and slather themselves with scented body oil before they leave the house. Men dot candles around the sitting room and change the sheets. There's nothing impromptu or unplanned about it.

Fight boredom by becoming in some sense a stranger to him again, in and out of the bedroom. Maintain a little independence and aloofness. Make him wonder who you really are. Don't just go to see the movies he wants to see. Go on trips, even if he doesn't want to go. Create some freedom from each other, so you have something to talk about when you meet again.

Bring some adventure back home. Email him with your sexual fantasies. Ask him about his. Don't pee in front of him. Wear make-up just for him. Learn a new skill without telling him. Give him something new to discover. Don't ever let yourself be entirely *known*.

S.W.A.L.K.

How many times have you bitched to your girlfriends that your man isn't romantic any more? He doesn't buy you flowers. He only remembers your anniversary if you drop heavy hints for a solid month beforehand. The only time he runs your bath and lights the scented candles is when he wants sex.

Well, girls, I've got news for you. Men *are* romantic. It's *women* who aren't.

We've lost the art of romancing our husbands. We think it's all about *them* coming to *us*. We hang around our towers waiting for Prince Charming to scale the wall without even thinking about throwing him down a rope.

Men may take the active role, but it's up to us to take a *pro*active one. Our job isn't to sit around passively waiting for him to write us a love poem or plant our names in daffodils in the front garden. It's to create an environment where romance will flourish and take root.

Part of that is, yes, dressing the part. Answer the door to him in a pair of old sweats and carpet slippers, and you'll be treated like The Wife. Open it dressed in a curve-skimming jersey wrap and kitten heels (the most impractical and annoying shoe ever devised, fit *only* for opening doors in; certainly not for walking), and you'll be treated like The Lover.

Old-fashioned? Demeaning? Tell me, why is wanting to be sexy and attractive for your man so out of favour these days?

Women may have decided that sexy isn't a figure-hugging skirt and some high heels any more. Unfortunately, no one told the men.

There's a world of difference between being loved for who you are (and trust me, he *really* doesn't notice that extra ten pounds, so quit worrying) and defiantly 'letting yourself go', as it used to be known.

It's as if some women *dare* their husbands to stray. *You fell in love with a pretty girl with long hair who wore short skirts and lashings of red lipstick*, they say, *so now I'm going to crop my hair into an unflattering military crew cut, pile on three stone and storm around in shapeless jeans and oversized sweaters. Now love me. Go on. I dare you.*

Act like a lover. Why should it be men who buy flowers? Why not you?

Send them to the office; apart from anything else, it'll throw the cat amongst the pigeons if the Bitch is someone who works with him. Hard for him to argue that you lead separate lives and neglect him if you're filling every available workspace with American Beauties and delphiniums.

While you're at it, send him a card with something wickedly intimate written inside. Post it to his office; or, even better, the hotel he's staying at when he's away on business. (She's *never* going to believe you two aren't sleeping together when she sees it.)

Never underestimate the guilt factor. If you're being so nice and thoughtful that it's almost as if you're not actually married, he's going to feel even more of a heel for sneaking off to see someone else. He'll start to wonder if it's worth it. With you covering all the bases, what does the Bitch have to offer?

Co-opt your friends into babysitting the kids, and book a weekend away. Yes, it's a cliché, but it works. If nothing else, it'll drive the Bitch crazy when she finds out; and trust me, she will.

Set up a date night for the two of you every week. Don't let him duck it with excuses; subtly play on his guilt and terror of being caught, and he'll be putty in your hands. Once you've got him on the other side of the restaurant table, flirt with him. Engage him in conversation. Avoid talking about the kids, the bills, or whether the boiler needs fixing. *Seduce* him. Remember how that works? (Oh yes, you do. It's like riding a bike. You'd remember if Hugh Jackman was in the building in double quick time.)

And at the end of the night, go home and have athletic, energetic, rambunctious sex.

Whose trousers are these, anyway?

Women think of male romance in terms of gifts or actions – flowers, dinners out – but for men romance is not about what you buy or do so much as how you present yourself to him – hence the importance of the seamed stockings and lippy – and how you reinforce his ego by treating him as sexy and heroic and all-conquering.

Treat him like a man, rather than an extra child, and he will act like one.

Let him finish a sentence without you constantly interrupting. Permit him to organize the fridge his way. Allow him to be the man in your relationship, and you'll be treated like the woman – as opposed to the cleaner, the cook and the nanny.

I'm not saying you should walk backwards in front of him or cater to his every whim. But we women have become so contemptuous of men in general that we undermine and disrespect them without even realizing it, and we bring that attitude home. Gather a bunch of women together and they'll start man-bashing before the first bottle of Chablis has been emptied. Men don't do this. Men are not bitches (small 'b').

You need to look at him with new eyes: *her* eyes. See him not as a breadwinner or father or rival for Most Stressed Working Parent award, but as a person with feelings and fears, hopes and dreams, opinions and needs. Don't stamp all over them.

Show him some respect in his own home. Don't diss him in front of the kids. Accept that his way won't always be your way, but it's probably just as good.

'I'd been married to Lance for about six years when I started suspecting he was having an affair. It was nothing specific; just a hunch. He was working later than usual, he seemed distracted at home, and he was always disappearing to make phone calls in his study.

'You'd think I'd feel devastated or angry, but instead I felt challenged. Things had got a bit boring with Lance, and I'd stopped really noticing him, but thinking someone else was after him made me look at him differently.

'We were out with friends one night, and something someone said made Lance throw his head back and roar with laughter. I realized it'd been months since I'd even seen him smile at something I'd said.

'I didn't want to ask him outright if he was having an affair, because Lance is the kind of person who'll cut off his nose to spite his face if he's thrown on to the defensive. I didn't want to back him into a corner. Instead, I started to make more effort to make him the centre of attention when he was home. We began to talk more. I was shocked when Lance said he felt really lonely, like I wasn't really seeing him at all. I realized how much I'd been ignoring him, like he was a room-mate or lodger rather than my husband. I started to spend less time at the gym or out with friends, and we agreed to go out on our own together once a week. We met up for lunch – I'd stop by his office, and kiss him in public and generally make it clear to anyone who was watching how much of a couple we were.

'Lance lapped up the attention. The late nights at work stopped almost immediately, and it felt like he was back again. There wasn't any room for anyone else in his life. That was three years ago, and things are so much better now, it's like it was when we were newlyweds.

'I've still never asked him if he was unfaithful. I don't want to know.'

Marie, 36, PA

Remember the line from *Love Story* about love meaning never having to say you're sorry? Bullshit. Love means having to say you're sorry *often*. Yes, even when you're in the right.

Home advantage

Let's be absolutely clear about one thing, just in case you're in any doubt. This is *not* the time to play fair, be considerate, share and share alike, or let the best woman win. All's fair in love and war. I don't want you growing compunction or a conscience now.

She may be the new pussy, damn her, but *you've* got home advantage.

Most men don't want to leave their wives. They're too lazy, it's too expensive and they love their families – including you. It's extremely hard to persuade a man to up sticks unless he's really convinced he's got nothing to lose. Which means you don't have to do too much to tip the balance in your favour. Take care of yourself, take care of him; and play a little dirty when it comes to taking care of her.

A man having an affair doesn't just lie to his wife. He lies to the Bitch too. Whatever bullshit he's feeding you, she's getting a double helping.

My wife and I lead separate lives. We haven't slept together since our youngest was born. I'll leave as soon as the children are both at school.

Blah, blah, blah. The point is, all women know married men almost never leave their wives. When the Bitch has an affair with one, she convinces herself that she'll be among the tiny fraction for whom it all works out. (Though why she'd think that landing a man who's just abandoned his young family and the woman he promised to love for ever is a result, I can't imagine.) But deep down, she knows the odds are stacked against her.

The Bitch won't admit it, even to herself, but she's as insecure as hell. And with good reason: she's actually got far more to worry about than you. She knows you hold pretty much all the cards. She's terrified you'll crook your little finger and he'll run home, his tail between his legs.

All you have to do is prey on that insecurity and your job is done.

Few things are more satisfying than sowing discord between a man and his Bitch. And there are so many *deliciously* wicked ways you can do it.

We've already touched on a few. Make sure everyone around you – especially his work colleagues – sees just how loved up the two of you are. Get a great photo of the two of you and have it framed for his office. Drop in as often as you can get away with, and make sure you get in plenty of tongue action in full public view.

Chatter gaily to his secretary about how *exhausted* you are (nudge nudge) after last night.

Ruin their dates and romantic trysts by changing your plans at the last minute. Nothing kills the moment like disappointment – and she's far more likely to say something she'll regret to him when she's pissed off because he's had to cancel again.

So, stay home when he thought you were going to be out. Don't go away for that weekend with the girls you've had in the diary for months. (Bang goes his romantic trip to Paris.)

Suddenly decide to come along with him when he goes off

on an errand, and don't take no for an answer.

Invite friends over for Sunday lunch, sabotaging his plans to 'play golf'. Nonchalantly let him know you might 'pop home one day this week' during the workday to catch up on things, thus scuppering any idea he might have had about bringing the Bitch back for a quickie.

Without sounding in the least suspicious – you don't want to alert him, remember – casually mention that you've been checking the phone bill because it's been so high recently, or that you've been keeping an eye on the credit-card bill because there are so many cases of fraud these days. He'll be forced to resort to yet more subterfuge just in case you spot something you shouldn't, and the added strain as the deceit piles up may make him decide it's not worth the candle.

Men are inherently lazy. A considerable part of the lure of a Bitch is that she makes things easy for him: no-strings sex, no nagging, no baggage. A little sneaking around is exciting, but if he has to work too hard for it . . . well, quite simply, he won't.

Unless the Bitch is a career mistress – unlikely if your man isn't fairly wealthy – she's not in this for fun. She thinks he loves her; her endgame is to have him leave you for her.

Things may be tense and strained between you and your man at home (though if you act on some of my recommendations in this chapter that should soon change) but *she* doesn't have to know that. The weekend plans together, your sexy text messages to his phone – yes, *of course* she looks through it when he's not looking, same as you do – the family holiday in Spain, the flowers and phone calls and new shirts; she'll see all of it as proof that, contrary to the line he's been spinning her, his wife *does* understand him. From which she'll infer that his wife sleeps with him too.

As the evidence mounts, she'll get crosser and crosser. She'll push him more and more to leave you. He'll start to feel pressured and defensive. In the end, they'll spend so much time rowing over you, they won't have time to get jiggy.

Which is what we call a Result.

How *could* you?

You may get to a point when you feel you simply have to confront him. As with everything else, there's a time and a place for this if you want to emerge in control of the situation.

The time is when you're quite sure you're ready, emotionally and financially. Only you can determine the former. For the latter, turn to Chapter Twelve: Don't Get Mad, Get Diamonds. It'll tell you all you need to know.

The place is *not* in front of your children. It's not over the kitchen counter as you scream and yell things that you will never be able to take back. It isn't when either of you is tired, or angry, or drunk.

Be sure you have the time and space for this conversation to last for as long as it needs to, and that you won't be interrupted. Take the phone off the hook.

Gather your evidence, so that he can't wrong-foot you by denying it. Be sure you're really ready; hearing it from his own lips is so much worse than a phone number on a printed page.

Be quite certain you're prepared for him to leave or stay.

This is the moment of truth. You stand at a crossroads, and there's no real way to know which way you'll be facing when the conversation is over.

Hard as it is, you need to keep your cool and your wits about you.

When you ask him questions, be firm, rather than tentative. Don't allow him to pick up the subliminal message that you don't really want to know. It's easier to rip the sticking plaster off in one fell swoop, rather than have him tell you 'It was only once' and then discover, in three weeks' time, that what he *really* meant was 'It was only once a week'.

Don't threaten to leave, or demand that he moves out. Don't attack him. It'll only put him on the defensive, and then he may do or say things he regrets.

Don't blame him, but don't let him turn the attack on you and come up with a list of excuses for his behaviour.

Don't expect one conversation to solve everything. This is just the beginning. It'll take time to re-establish trust, but it will be worth the effort if it gives you a better marriage; and, yes, even if it gives you a better divorce.

Keep the focus on you and your man, not the Bitch. Minimize her importance by giving as little attention as possible to who, where and when. You can find these things out later, if you really want to know. The last thing you need is for him to spring to her defence.

At the end of the day, this isn't about her. It's about the two of you.

Perhaps more importantly than anything, don't do all the talking. You wouldn't be in this situation if the two of you were communicating well. So *listen to him.*

If he tells you he wants to stay married, believe him.

In a nutshell

Play to win. Either convert to Wicca, or:

1. Take care of you:
Kick-box her into touch
Nourish yourself
Soothe your soul

2. Take care of him:
Lots of inventive, energetic sex
Treat him like a man – a little respect goes
a long way
Channel your inner romantic

3. Take care of her:
Sabotage their time together
Prey on her insecurity
Use your home advantage

If and when you confront him:
Gather your evidence
Choose your moment
Don't threaten or attack him
Keep the focus on the two of you, not
the Bitch
Let him talk . . . and listen to him

Chapter Ten
Interview With a Vamp

Let me ask you a question:

Ever been paid for sex?

Oh, don't be so shocked. It's a perfectly reasonable thing to ask. You'd be surprised how often the answer is yes. But OK, I accept that statistically you probably haven't actually had someone write you a cheque or leave fifty-pound notes fanned on the bedside table. So let's make this a bit simpler. Have you ever gone out with a man you didn't fancy, simply because he was rich?

Been taken on an expensive date – five-star restaurant, tickets to a West End show, late-night martinis at a chic bar – and then slept with a man afterwards, not because you really wanted to, but because somehow you felt you *owed* him?

Continued seeing someone because he sent you extravagant bouquets and marked Valentine's Day and anniversaries with pale turquoise boxes from Tiffany?

Maybe you even went so far as to actually marry a man because he was a 'good catch' – right sort of job, right sort of income, right sort of friends – even though you never *quite* felt about him the way you did about that crazy, wild, unsuitable boy you dated at university. (Yes, the one you dumped because everyone said he'd never make anything of himself. The one who went on to become a celebrity photographer and is now worth millions.)

Fine line, isn't it?

Olivia is an attractive, articulate ex-convent girl in her early thirties with a First from Oxford. She speaks several languages fluently, and is well read and well travelled.

She's also a hooker.

Three years ago, following the end of a passionate affair with a married man (whose identity she still discreetly maintains; we'll call him Mr X), she gave up her corporate job to become the English Courtesan: a high-class call-girl with a string of influential, successful lovers whom she charges thousands of pounds a night.

I've spoken to a number of mistresses in researching this book, but all of them had an agenda. Olivia has none. She's better placed than anyone to tell us exactly why our men stray. And as she points out, all mistresses are paid for their services, in one form or another.

Olivia is simply being up-front about the cost of fucking her.

She knows precisely what errant husbands want from their wives, and aren't getting. What she has to say about married men and their needs is revealing and unbiased. If you think I've been too old-fashioned in the preceding chapter or two, you should listen *very carefully* to what she has to say.

Man's nature to stray

I used to think that an affair meant there was something wrong in a marriage or that a wife had in some way 'failed' her husband. I'm snorting with laughter at my own naïvety on that. It's in a man's nature to stray.

I can honestly say that every man I know, without exception, has at one point or another been unfaithful to a girlfriend or wife. Friends, neighbours, colleagues; I can't name a single man who hasn't cheated.

Escorting has confirmed my belief that whatever a woman does, there's a very good chance that her partner will stray. Some of the clients I see have what one might consider an 'excuse', be it a wife who's permanently cross, a wife who hits them or is verbally or emotionally abusive, or a wife who doesn't like sex. A few have other reasons for staying in an unhappy marriage, such as a disabled child, or a business that they can't bear to see sold for a divorce settlement. I feel only sympathy and regret for these men. They don't see a way out and so they see me as an alternative to breaking up their marriage.

Yet there are also several clients I see who have no real reason at all to see an escort and who profess to love their wives. By their own account, they have happy marriages, a good sex life, a wife who loves them and whom they love. I've got one at the moment who wants to meet me but who's busy telling me all about his lingerie shopping trips with his wife, how she loves choosing things he'll like and how he loves treating her to them, how she likes lace, how she wears cotton nighties in bed, how she only started shaving in her forties, etc., etc. I'm appalled at the intimate details he's telling me – she'd be mortified, just as I would if he were my partner. If his sex life is this good, what on earth does he think he's doing writing to me?

Meeting Mr X

I became a courtesan directly because of Mr X. I don't hold him responsible for that, but I'd never have thought of this otherwise. My logic was that I was a good mistress so I might as well be paid for it. I was loving and kind, attentive and loyal, and I made him feel good about himself. Those things weren't an effort – they're who I am – but other things were, like learning not to ask questions, and to walk past hotel receptions with my head held high. I might as well put those skills to good use.

[The affair] began when I flew out to Sri Lanka for Christmas. On the first morning, as I was having a leisurely breakfast, a man came up to my table. He had been sitting with an impeccable-looking blonde woman in a distinctly frosty silence. He looked to be in his late fifties and had grey hair, sparkling eyes and a certain je ne sais quoi about him.

Over the next two weeks, I became friends with Mr and Mrs X. I was aware his marriage was not a happy one from the minor spats I witnessed. He never raised the subject, but there was evident misery in the little things.

We all flew home, having agreed that we would meet again the following year. We again spent an enjoyable and lazy two weeks. Nothing had happened between myself and Mr X at this point, but [after the holiday] we met in London. He told me his marriage was over and that I was his soulmate. Like the incurable romantic that I am, I believed him, and soon after that I became his mistress. Thus began a two-year affair.

No limits

Our experimentation knew no limits, and he could ask of his mistress things that he would never have dared ask of his wife. We christened every imaginable location, indoors and out. I will never forget my first sight of his giant erection when he emerged warm and damp from the shower and I pulled away his little white towel. That is my memory of Kobe. Or the sudden, sharp, animal sex in a stone circle up on the windswept moors one hot summer's afternoon. That was Derbyshire. Or straddling his wide, warm body to lick iced plum juice off his nipples and then moving slowly down, hidden by the balcony balustrades. That was Riva del Garda. Or the delights of spinning together naked, me sitting in his lap rodeo style, on the big black revolving leather chair in his office.

It's not that I didn't think of Mrs X, and indeed I was consumed by guilt. Mrs X was a woman with whom I might have been friends in another life. We read the same books, liked the same art, cried at the same films, liked the same food. Later I discovered he took us to the same hotels, told us the same anecdotes about his working life and bought us the same perfume, presumably so that we wouldn't smell each other on him. By the time I realized he had no intention of leaving, it was too late and I loved him.

The man of my dreams

Perhaps it was the fact that when I met him he seemed a little sad and lost and world-weary. With me he was a different man – his whole body language and demeanour changed. By her side, as when I first met him, he stooped and shuffled, but with me he stood up straight and strode and sparkled. He often spoke of how bored he was with his life, and with me he seemed to rediscover his inner child and see his world through fresh eyes.

He once said that it was only the thought of me that made his life with her bearable. I wonder now if that was all an illusion, but I felt at the time that I could make him happy, just as he made me happy.

At our first meeting back in the UK, he told me that I was the woman of his dreams, the English rose he'd been looking for all his life, and that his marriage was over. He said he didn't love his wife and was about to divorce. It took him just a week to say he loved me, although it took me a little longer to reciprocate. On our first trip away, he told me it would take him a while to 'sort things out' but that he would be with me properly if I would just give him a little time.

Layers of lies

'A little time' stretched out and before I knew it it was a year, then two. Each time I despaired, there was a little progress – he applied for a job near where I live, persuaded me to put in an offer on a house for us, talked about what our children would be like.

Mr X was also a bit of an onion, in that it was only after about a year that his layers of lies gradually emerged. When he didn't leave as he'd promised I started to question whether he ever would, but by that stage I loved him and I didn't know how to sort things out. I broke it off several times, but each time he'd eventually call or write and I'd forgive him again. Perhaps it's true that love is a form of insanity. I still hoped beyond hope and I suppose I trusted him.

At that point, what he told me started to unravel – he admitted that he was sleeping with his wife (he'd said he wasn't), that he'd been on several holidays with her (one notable incident was when he claimed to be working in the US but I checked and discovered he was in Greece on holiday with her), etc. etc. When he told me that he loved her, almost two years after we'd met, I was genuinely shocked.

I knew he called [Mrs X] twice a day, but he said that was 'to avoid suspicion' and he called me twice a day too. It was only later that I realized he used the same pet names for us both, bought us the same perfume, cooked us the same food, and went on holiday with [Mrs X], when he had told me he was alone on work trips. We went shopping together and I helped him choose clothes for himself and gifts for [her]. [Their] house and his office are full of the gifts I bought him – the digital radio in his workshop, the set of silver pencils and the card box [Mrs X uses] for bridge, the Liberty spoons [she serves] coffee with afterwards, the first editions of Keats in his study. Ironically she was more of a kept woman than I ever was or ever will be.

An old carpet slipper

She got her man and in a way I'm glad of that. If she does divorce him, I hope she'll do it on her own terms and that she'll be happy. As for him, even there I find it hard to be angry. He once said desperately that he'd overestimated his ability to leave her, and I think that was true in a way. He is due to retire in two years and in his first divorce he lost his home, so I can understand that he doesn't want to lose it all a second time round. Their life is comfortable – he once described her as 'a bit like an old carpet slipper' and I think she probably views him in the same light. It's not an exciting life but it works, whereas I would have been an unknown. I'd have gambled it all for him, but perhaps we weren't as alike as I once thought.

I've caused a lot of pain and that was never my intention – I'd never even cheated on anyone before [Mr X], let alone slept with someone married. I'd never ever have got involved if it weren't for the fact that at the outset he told me his marriage was over, and had been over since his wife's affair about a year before we met. His wife hates me, and I understand that, but I could never hate her. I'm deeply sorry and appalled at what I've done and I genuinely never set out to break up their marriage.

An affair leaves total devastation all round – for the man, for the wife and for the mistress. No one comes out of it 'stronger' – one woman has to triumph over the other in the end and the man is likely to spend the rest of his married life in the doghouse. Courtesans offer a more symbiotic relationship. One client told me his wife was fully aware of him seeing me and 'might even be interested in joining us one day'.

Unconditional love

I enjoy my new life. I like men and they like me. [They] seem to fit a particular mould – clever, successful and usually married. Sex is admittedly a major part of it, but it's not just about sex, despite what people think. Nor is it about looks. I'm attractive, a size eight to ten, 34B with long wavy hair and big eyes, but I'm not a supermodel and that's not why clients choose me.

The sad fact is that a long-term partner will never compete with an escort. Real women don't want to give four hours of oral sex or to listen to their man talk at, rather than to, them for three hours without a breath. Real women get tired, have stresses, get PMT, have bristly legs occasionally, etc. I don't think any woman could maintain [an escort's] level of care in a permanent relationship. The energy levels men require from an escort are superhuman. I often find I have to just sleep for hours and hours, both before and after a booking. It's not just physical, it's emotional exhaustion. Sometimes I come home feeling utterly battered, sexually and psychologically. My clients are really nice men and I'm not complaining – my job is to give them what they need and I'm handsomely paid for it. Yet what I'm saying is that I don't think there's any way a long-term partner could offer that day in, day out.

Their wives for the most part have lost interest in them, so what my clients want is someone who makes them feel special, someone who makes them feel clever and attractive. They want someone who'll listen to them, who'll take an interest in what they do, who'll care if they're sad or ill. It's a combination of lover and friend and mother, I think, that all-embracing, non-judgemental affection. If I were to sum up what they want most, it's unconditional love.

Left behind

One thing strikes me about the marriages of the clients I've seen to date and it's that these are men who have married 'beneath them' in some way. That sounds such a horribly old-fashioned phrase but I don't quite know how else to put it. They have married women who are from less affluent or educated backgrounds. Since their marriage, these women have either become ladies who lunch or they continue to work in caring professions – they are primary-school teachers or nurses – and they carry on working not out of financial need but because they enjoy it.

I don't quite understand why it is that these men choose wives with whom they quickly discover they have nothing in common. I can only assume that they were drawn to 'nurturing' women who they thought would make good mothers. I suppose too that, if you're an alpha male, then you don't necessarily want another one at home. Perhaps it's also the business about the higher your IQ, the less likely you are to find a mate if you're female. It seems deeply sad somehow that whilst these men have moved on since marrying, in terms of continuing their education, building their global empires and developing sophisticated tastes in all things, their wives have been left behind. The men wanted their wives to be good mothers, but now that they've become that, they find them boring and narrow-minded. I think that's why they like me – they've forgotten what it's like to have interesting pillow talk with someone who regards them as an equal rather than a superior.

A straight transaction

I'm struck by the fact that none of my clients to date have been people who have to pay for sex. These are witty, charming and attractive men and there would undoubtedly be plenty of women willing to have affairs with them. Yet in an odd way they're also honest people and I think that's part of why they choose to see me – it's less risky than an affair and they can be confident that I'll never ring up their wife in a rage. For them this is very much a choice, and a carefully considered one at that.

They're all successful in their chosen fields and they tend to be highly educated. Most are from corporate backgrounds, banking or the tech sector, or they have their own companies. All are in positions where regular travel does not arouse suspicions. They range in age from thirties to early sixties. They do tell me about their marriages and their children too, but much of what they tell me is about work. They ask my advice on all sorts of things, from what to buy their wife for Christmas to whether they should take over a rival company.

My clients like the fact that they can talk to me as an equal, in that my background is the corporate world from which most of them come. I think they like the fact that they can be honest with me too and they tell me things that they could never tell their wife or their work colleagues. In a strange way, I'm more trustworthy than an unpaid mistress – I'll never betray a confidence, I'll never get jealous and I'll never fall in love with them. My background, appearance and education mean that, as I say on my blog, 'no one will ever suspect me of being anything other than a good catch'. I have Mr X to thank for that – I often went away with him on work trips and no one ever seemed to question who or what I was.

What [men] like in a courtesan – wit and kindness and charm and intelligence and independence – are not what they want in a wife. They like an equal in the bedroom and in the boardroom, but they don't want one at home.

www.englishcourtesan.blogspot.com

So what do we take from this, other than a sudden craving for razor blades and a hundred paracetamol?

Well, first of all, becoming a courtesan probably isn't the swiftest path to true love. Women like Olivia attract a certain type of man. The cheating kind, to be frank.

She's seen too much of the seamier side of human relationships. She's fallen prey to a very modern disease. A cynic, Oscar Wilde said, is a man (or woman) who knows the price of everything and the value of nothing.

Maybe real women can't maintain the same levels of attention and energy 24/7 that a call-girl can muster for a few hours a week. But a hooker can't tell a client she loves him, and mean it.

Men don't expect us to be perfect. They don't actually expect sex on tap, or for you to wash their feet with your tears and dry them with your hair.

Give them a little love and affection, and throw in a few numbers from the next chapter now and again, and they'll be yours for ever.

Chapter Eleven
Ten Things Men Really Like in Bed

1. Blow-jobs

'The world is divided into two types of men: those who love blow-jobs, and those who are dead. Nothing is sexier than a dirty bitch rubbing your cum into her face after sex.'

Chris, 32, lawyer

2. Finger up the arse

'I love it when a woman puts her finger up my arse and sucks me off at the same time. If she can manage to gently squeeze and juggle my balls at the same time, so much the better.'

Will, 28, mason

3. Talking dirty

'Dirty talk. Some eye contact while she's sucking my cock is good, as are occasional feats of swallowing/accepting a facial. I want her to have a trimmed, pleasant-looking cunt. And firm breasts, size not so important. No odours, obviously. Someone who I can 'make love to' as well as treat like a French whore while bent over the sofa having her hair pulled. The occasional episode of lesbianism is also a perfect birthday treat.'   *James, 47, TV presenter*

4. Playing with herself

'I like watching a girl play with herself, and two girls together (of course!). A woman who really gets involved and enjoys herself; who's not afraid to be slutty.'

Luke, 37, entrepreneur

5. Dressing up

'I really like it when she dresses up for me. Convent schoolgirl is my favourite, but a pair of nice lacy knickers and a push-up bra with suspenders and stockings works too, It's not just about her looking horny, it's the fact that she's bothered to go to the trouble. It's like she's saying she wants it as much as you do.'   *Terry, 29, photographer*

6. Anal sex

'Anal sex. A woman's cunt just isn't as tight, especially after she's had kids. It makes me horny just talking about it. I'm attracted to strong intelligent women with a sharp sense of humour and to women with a streak of recklessness. Giving it up the arse to a woman like that is a real turn-on.'

Charles, 60, civil servant

7. Fucking from behind

'My ultimate fuck is a 'three holer' – mouth, pussy and arse to finish. I like fucking from behind especially. I don't know whether this is because we've been together so long I don't have to look at her face (and so can fantasize about other women), but she has a fine arse and I am a bit of a voyeur. I enjoy the fact my wife has a fantastic body that I can look at while we're having sex.'   *Damian, 43, scriptwriter*

8. The risk of discovery

'New places and situations are a key trigger. The danger element, the risk of discovery, is a great turn-on. I like being propositioned, the flash of an eye, a series of texts during the day, a promise of what is to come. Walking in the door and finding her in any kind of compromising position, like sitting at the bottom of the stairs with a smile (and no knickers). In bed I like to lick, I like to hear the passion rising, to be given verbal encouragement . . . "Mmm, there please, a little harder, faster, use your fingers . . ."'

Simon, 42, manager

9. Sharing fantasies

'When a woman writes her fantasy down and emails it to you, or reads it to you in bed. A good friend once videoed herself and when she saw my reaction she secretly borrowed my Dictaphone to record her fantasy while making herself come. The audio was much more powerful than the video.'

Nick, 34, TV producer

10. Taking charge

'I hate girls who get all girly and coy in the sack, like they're retread virgins. I like a woman who takes the initiative in bed, and doesn't wait for me to make all the moves. It's such a bore having to figure out what she wants; it makes life so much easier if she'll just tell you, or better yet, get on with it herself. Nothing's sexier than a woman flinging *you* around the room from one position to the next, and once you can quit worrying if you're satisfying her, you're free to please yourself.'   *Andy, 35, investment analyst*

*

Obviously you don't have to push the boat out quite this far every time (or hit all ten in one night . . . not unless you want to fuck the poor chap to death) but perhaps adding a little variety to your repertoire and treating him more than once a year on his birthday would be nice.

Chapter Twelve
Don't Get Mad, Get Diamonds

There may come a point when you can ride the train no further. Maybe you simply can't bear to live with him any more, despite your best efforts. Perhaps he's determined on divorce. I ache for you, truly I do. But if it has to happen, let's at least make sure that you come out on top. It's your turn, after all.

When my husband left me, I made one crucial detour *en route* to the divorce lawyer's office. To a jeweller, where I emptied our joint savings account in return for a £35,000 pair of three-carat diamond earrings.

Clever? No (though other deserted wives should bear in mind that jewellery is rarely taken into account in a divorce settlement). Satisfying? Yes, immensely.

Right now, nothing can anaesthetize the pain you're experiencing. Betrayal lacerates your heart, your soul, your pride and your sense of self, and even when the wound has long since healed, there will be times it'll *still* sting like a son of a bitch. It's ten years since my husband left, and I'm now happily remarried to a man I adore; yet I still wince when I remember the pain of those early days.

But it *is* only a memory. It doesn't hurt *now*. The reason for that – essentially the difference between healing and moving forward, or just surviving, trapped in the past – is a Good Divorce.

Oh yes, and those diamonds.

My first port of call the day he walked out was a friend who'd been through the same thing herself a year or two before. She came over, listened patiently for about twenty minutes, then picked up her bag, handed me my coat and shepherded me out of the door.

'I know this amazing place,' she said firmly, 'it always makes me feel better. Trust me, ten minutes in there and you'll feel like a different woman.'

Tearfully I followed her, expecting her to take me to some sort of spa: aromatherapy and hot stones, soothing massage and sweet-smelling unguents. Perhaps a church for some spiritual comfort; or maybe the beach for a breathtaking view across the Mediterranean (I lived in Lebanon at the time), nature in all its wonder rendering my petty problems insignificant and irrelevant.

Maybe even a therapist; the one must-have accessory I didn't have (and, given my state of mind, really should have had).

Instead, she frogmarched me to her friend's jewellery shop across town.

'Diamonds,' she ordered peremptorily, 'two carats, I think.'

The dealer produced a tray of glittering, sparkling, dazzling, shimmering, magnificent unset diamonds.

(Possibly the only thing that distracted me from his extreme, and I do mean *extreme,* sexiness. When I had my not-to-be-recommended retaliatory affair, handily enough it was with the aforementioned diamond dealer.)

As my girlfriend explained, diamonds would do three things for me. First, it'd 'hit the bastard where it hurt' – in the wallet – and make me feel a helluva lot better. Diamonds just do that for a girl.

Second, it'd be some sort of insurance if he suddenly evaporated in a puff of smoke and I was left without any visible means of support. My sons were only four and one at the time; I was hardly in a position to earn my way quite yet. As my smart friend pointed out, if things ever got desperate, a good pair of diamond earrings would pay the boys' school fees for several years.

And, third, it'd take a large chunk of cash out of marital circulation and put it firmly on my side of the books.

When a couple split up, all their assets go into a marital pot. House, cars, cash, pension, savings: in it all goes. Whatever your lawyer tells you about reasonable needs and maintaining your standard of living, how that pot gets split depends primarily on the mood of the judge on the day, and whether he (or she) got laid the night before.

It *isn't* fair. Right doesn't always triumph. Frankly, it's a bloody lottery.

In theory, jewellery should also get counted as part of the marital assets. In practice, unless you own a collection of gems that includes Wallis Simpson's tiara, possession is nine-tenths of the law. A bracelet is only worth what you can get for it, not what it cost, and most judges are very reluctant to get into a blow-by-blow, necklace-by-earring division of spoils.

Which means that the diamond earrings are yours.

So I settled on a stunning pair of two-carat studs, and wrote out an exhilarating cheque with lots of zeros on our joint account.

Later that night, I was with my friend and the sexy diamond dealer in a restaurant when my husband called from the other side of the world, where he was supposedly working. I knew he was really with *her*, though of course he had no idea I'd rumbled him.

Let's just say the conversation didn't go well. Put it this way: when it ended, I turned to the jeweller and told him to cancel the cheque. 'I'll be coming by your shop tomorrow to write out a new one,' I said furiously, 'for *three*-carat earrings.'

No more Mrs Nice Guy

As I've explained in previous chapters, the window between discovering his affair, and letting him know *you* know is absolutely crucial for multiple reasons, not least of which is the chance to position yourself advantageously if the worst comes to the worst and you end up staring divorce in the face.

This isn't about revenge (well, not entirely). It's about *survival*.

I truly hope it doesn't come to this for you. Many marriages can be saved, and end up not as they were before, but stronger, *better*. Fingers crossed this is the case with you.

But sometimes the only way to beat the Bitch is to let her have him. There are times when staying with him simply isn't an option; either because he's determined to rebuff you at every turn, or because you decide, as I did, that you simply don't want him enough to make the effort.

Only you can decide if you've reached that point. I'm not going to tell you which way to jump; my job is merely to point out that you do have options. Infidelity doesn't have to end in divorce.

But if divorce is inevitable for you, make sure it's a killer.

Money may not matter to you right now. You'd probably trade every penny you have for this not to have happened – I'd have swallowed those diamonds whole if I thought I could turn back the clock, for it all to have been a silly misunderstanding.

You couldn't care less about the roof over your head, when he's not going to be under it with you. But as my grandmother would say, wishful thinking never buttered no parsnips. This isn't the time to sob into your pillow and listen to maudlin love songs (I'm firmly of the opinion Nilsson's 'Without You' should be put on the same proscribed list as Class A drugs and semi-automatics). Feel sorry for yourself later. Right now, you need to toughen up and get with the programme.

I'm not suggesting you become one of those harpies determined to take him to the cleaners and leave him with nothing but the shirt on his back. First, it won't make you happy; and second, it'll destroy any chance you may have had to establish a decent working relationship as joint parents to your children.

But by the same token, your kids don't deserve to be short-changed just because the Bitch has come along ready to lay a few cuckoos.

I'm not going to sugar-coat it. You now have the fight of your life on your hands.

Forget the urban legend that women emerge from a divorce dripping in bling and in far better financial shape than men. Yes, the odd footballer's wife may walk off with a wheelbarrow of cash after an eighteen-month marriage and no kids, but it's not the norm.

Statistically men end up 25 per cent better off post-divorce than they were when they were married – principally because they're now keeping the lion's share of their income. Even if you're getting half, which frankly is unlikely, you'll have to use it to support yourself *and* the kids. Which is why, on average, women end up 20 per cent *worse* off after a divorce.

Suits and separates

Things aren't going to carry on as before, whatever he promises now to salve his conscience or get you off his back. Even if the guilty prick means it at the time, he's kidding himself. You're *separating*. That means two *separate* houses instead of one, two *separate* sets of water and electricity bills, twice the *separate* expenses. Never mind what happens if and when he starts another family with the Bitch.

Wise up, girlfriend.

This isn't something you can 'sort out between you' – though if I had a euro for every time I've heard a man use that line as he tries to persuade his wife to commit financial suicide, I'd be writing this on the sun-drenched balcony of a villa in Tuscany.

Once he leaves, it's all going to get very ugly very fast. He's *not* going to sit down at the kitchen table to go through all the finances with you nicely and show you what he's stashed where. The second the door shuts behind him as he leaves, you're the enemy. Whatever you may think, whatever he may tell you now, there's no such thing as an amicable divorce.

Let me say that again, larger this time:

THERE'S NO SUCH THING AS AN AMICABLE DIVORCE.

If you were able to get along and sort things out reasonably, you wouldn't be getting a bloody divorce in the first place.

Forget mediation, forget being nice to each other for the sake of the children (pfff!), forget his version of splitting things 'fairly'. Not that these aren't good things. In theory. It's just that *it's not going to work out that way*.

Not all lawyers belong at the bottom of the sea

Women are programmed to please. It's in our genes. We're tailor-made to keep the peace, and make our man happy.

This trait often comes to the fore in the immediate aftermath of a break-up, especially if you think, subconsciously or otherwise, that by being reasonable and mature and accommodating, you'll get him to come back to you. *He won't*.

What he *will* do is railroad you into an agreement that leaves you significantly worse off than you were when you were married, and with far less than you and/or the children are entitled to. Later, when the dust settles and you realize you've been taken for a ride, this is going to eat into your soul. The bitterness of a bad divorce lingers for years, if not decades.

This is the rest of your life we're talking about. Getting out of your marriage with a fair share of your *joint* (let's not forget that word) assets will mean the difference between a fresh start and a life lived in the shadows.

Before you do anything else, and certainly before you confront him, *get a lawyer*.

This is a scary thing to do, because it makes everything seem so final, but it in no way commits you to getting a divorce. When you view a house, you don't have to buy it. No more do you have to get a divorce just because you see a lawyer. But a friend of mine who thought she and her husband were 'working through' their problems was served out of the blue with a batch of terrifying documents and the closure of all their joint bank accounts and credit cards. Finding a lawyer in that kind of panic is doubly hard. Do it right away.

Too many women trust their husband when he insists they don't need a lawyer of their own. His lawyer will 'do all the paperwork', he says breezily, to 'save throwing money down the drain on two sets of legal fees.' (Yes, this would be the same man they *trusted* to love them as long as they both should live, forsake all others and keep only unto her, etc., etc.)

Then they wonder why they're stuck in a two-up, two-down in Croydon while he's got a six-bedroom house in Hampstead with a Mercedes parked in the drive.

The best way to find a lawyer is through a friend's

recommendation. Don't use the chap who helped you buy your house. You need an experienced family-law firm. If you can't find one through word of mouth, look online, but don't be afraid to shop around. (Do you ever buy the first LBD you see without at least trying on half a dozen others?)

My personal recommendation? For what it's worth: Simon Pigott, of Levison Meltzer Pigott in London. A truly wonderful man who kept me sane and solvent throughout my divorce, and who is now a very dear friend.

It may sound obvious, but be sure you *like* your lawyer. He or she is going to do battle for you in the most personal area of your life, and you must be comfortable with, and trust, them. Don't be fobbed off with platitudes, patronized, insulted or made to feel a nuisance. You will be *paying* them to work for you. They may be the professional, but *you* are the customer.

A girlfriend of mine saw a man recommended by a recently divorced male friend and left his offices feeling guilty and responsible even though it was her husband who had left her for his PA. She then saw two more before settling on a fifty-five-year-old woman who reminded her of her old headmistress, and never looked back.

Equally important to remember, though, is that however nice they are your lawyer is *not your friend*. (Not until they're off the clock, anyway.) He or she is not your therapist, your priest, or your hairdresser. Every single time you call to vent about the latest insult or outrage committed by your soon-to-be ex, you will be charged. A lot. Up to £500 an hour. That's £125 for your fifteen-minute strop about his holiday with the Bitch in Mauritius. Your mother, on the other hand, is free. Even if she does have an annoying tendency to say, 'I told you so' rather a lot of the time.

The boring legal stuff

Until they start down this miserable road, most people don't have an idea what the nuts and bolts of a divorce involve. So here's a quick summary (a lawyer can fill in the blanks for you) of the type you'd get if you popped round to mine for a coffee and two packets of HobNobs. Or, more likely, a bottle or two of Chablis and a few G&Ts to wash it down.

First of all, under current law you can't get divorced until you've been married at least a year. You don't have to *live* with the bastard for the full twelve months if it all goes belly-up on your honeymoon, but you can't actually file for divorce until it's been a calendar year since you said 'I do'.

There is currently only one ground for divorce: the petitioner (the person asking for the divorce) must establish that the marriage has irretrievably broken down. And you're allowed to pick one of five reasons that this may have happened:

1. The respondent (yes, your bastard husband) has committed adultery
2. The shit's behaved in such a way you can't 'reasonably' be expected to live with him
3. He's deserted you for at least two continuous years
4. You've lived apart for at least two continuous years, if he agrees to the divorce

5. You've lived apart for at least five continuous years, if the bugger won't

There are variations on this theme, including 'nullity' (when he's already got a wife stashed up in Liverpool; or can't, and has never been able to, get it up), but if that's the case I suggest you put this book down and see your lawyer and Max Clifford, and not necessarily in that order.

If you're going for the Standard Divorce, No Optional Extras, you will have to pick one of the five reasons above. This is assuming *he* hasn't decided to divorce *you*, in which case the rules are still the same, you just get to play respondent.

Although the law provides for conduct to be taken into account when determining the financial division of assets, unless it's *extreme* – by which I mean stabbing your mother or turning tricks at King's Cross – it usually won't make any difference. He doesn't have to pay you more because he had an affair, much as you might want to take the bastard to the cleaners.

If he's been screwing around and you can prove it, it's pretty pointless for him to fight a petition based on adultery. But you don't have to mention the Bitch by name; you can just cite an 'unknown person' if you want to be insulting. Or you could brand her as a husband-stealing slapper. Up to you.

The only thing you should be aware of is that if you've carried on living with him for more than six months after you *found out* about the affair (not necessarily six months since it happened) you can't get him on adultery. Sorry. The clock's ticking on this one.

'Unreasonable behaviour' covers a multitude of sins. (I think the fact that he's a man should be cause enough, but the law is lagging slightly behind me on this one.)

If neither of you wants to wait the two years or cite adultery – don't forget, one day you may have to explain to your children why you got divorced – unreasonable behaviour is usually a good option. Most marriages contain enough within them to satisfy this criterion (tell me about it), and the two of you can always agree on terms before submitting a petition.

You can basically make this one stretch to cover pretty much anything: being a moody bugger and watching *Top Gear* 24/7 are reasons enough.

The remaining three grounds all require periods of time apart. Desertion is used fairly rarely, and the main difference between this and separation is the issue of consent. If he fucks off without a word when you pop out for a pint of milk, he's deserted you – unless you were cutting his dick off when he slept. If he has good cause to leave, you can't claim desertion.

If you agree to separate, he will then have to consent to your petition for divorce for you to be able to get one in two years. If he refuses, it will take five.

It's usually fairly easy to determine that you're living apart in the physical sense – one of you will move out. But if you decide to stay together in the matrimonial home while waiting out your two years (and with the housing market in the crapper, this is becoming more and more common), you must have 'separate households'.

Separate bedrooms is not enough – if you still cook for the family and eat your meals with him, you could be said to still be together.

If you really want a divorce, you will get one, and it's rare you'll have to wait five years. Likewise, if he really wants one from you in order to marry the Bitch, you can throw in a few delaying tactics, but it won't really get you far. He *will* get his divorce eventually. And in the mean time, the longer you contest it, the richer the lawyers will get.

Once your divorce petition has been accepted, you will be granted a Decree Nisi, or non-absolute ruling, i.e. a ruling by a court that does not have any force until such time as a particular condition is met. (Typically, the condition is that no new evidence or further petitions with a bearing on the case are introduced to the court.) Once it's met, the ruling becomes a Decree Absolute, and is binding. Although in theory these decrees can be as little as six weeks apart, in practice the gap is often longer, because it's best not to get a Decree Absolute until all financial affairs are in order.

There are often benefits payable to a spouse – life insurance, for example – that you would not be eligible to receive if your divorce had come through. If you are still arguing about finances you could lose out if he dies and you've already got the Decree Absolute.

There's one final option, which stops just short of a divorce, but deals pretty effectively with everything else, and that's a 'judicial separation'. This doesn't end your marriage, but will deal with financial matters and those relating to the children in much the same way as a full divorce. It's quite handy if you can't stand the sight of him right now, but don't want to shut the door for ever – particularly if, say, staying technically married entitles you to perks that arise out of his job, such as health- or life-insurance eligibility, or simply because your mother is a committed Roman

Catholic who will make your life hell over Sunday lunch if you get divorced. She'll probably get you petitioning the Pope for an annulment next.

That bitch Mother Teresa

As the divorce drags on, it *will* wear you down. Be prepared for that, and accept it. This isn't going to be a happy time for you. Suck it up, and think how good you're going to feel when it's all over.

Friends will probably tell you that you need to rise above it and let it go; that money doesn't buy happiness and it's not worth fighting over every saucepan; let him keep the stupid boat if it means you can draw a line under the whole thing and move on.

Well, yes. But however much we might want to take the moral high ground, it's hard to move on with your life when you're struggling to pay the rent, or get your ancient Fiat through its MoT.

As I said before, this isn't about revenge so much as survival. Practical survival, yes; but emotional and psychological survival too.

Being the 'better person' isn't quite so easy when you have to watch him swan off with the kids to Val d'Isère at half-term, or listen through gritted teeth as they excitedly regale you with their adventures at Disney World, while you don't even know how you're going to pay the next electricity bill.

Unless you're possessed of a sweetness of nature that would make Mother Teresa seem like a vengeful bitch, anger and resentment at a raw deal will eventually eat you up. Bitterness is an ugly emotion, and it'll fuck up your life.

10 common divorce mistakes

1. Thinking your ex will play fair. The court system is adversarial by nature. He's going to look out for number one, and so should you

2. Signing paperwork without understanding what it really means

3. Expecting too much. You won't get everything you want. Your assets are being split in two, so both of you are going to lose some ground

4. Letting your heart rule your head. Don't screw up a good deal because your emotions get in the way. Keep your cool and remember: this is business

5. Lying to your lawyer. Don't. They won't judge you, but they need to know everything if they're to look after your best interests

6. Expecting the judge to take your side when he hears what a bastard your husband has been to you. He won't. This is about facts, not emotion. Present a good case, and keep feelings out of it

7. Not verifying important figures independently. Don't trust your husband to tell the truth. Double-check everything, including your lawyer's information

8. Not getting independent financial advice. Lawyers aren't accountants. When you're dealing with pensions or complex trusts, get expert advice. You don't want to be hit with a huge tax bill years from now

9. Being late with legal papers. Courts take deadlines very seriously; so should you

10. Sweating the small stuff. Don't ring your lawyer every five minutes. It'll cost you time and money, and send your stress levels through the roof. Keep focused on the big picture

You don't need to rise above the fray. You just need to *win*.

On a purely practical level, how will you ever meet a new man (yes, one day you *will* want to, I promise) if you can never afford to go out, or pay for a babysitter? What happens to *your* prospects for a romantic weekend in Paris? How are you ever going to get that lovely sun-kissed glow if the only holiday you can afford is a weekend in Clacton?

'So many of my clients are terrified of upsetting their husband, even after he's emptied the savings account and run off with their sister,' says Carina Matthews, senior partner at a top London divorce firm. 'They don't want to seem demanding, or risk alienating him.

'I'll sit down and go through their day-to-day needs with them food, clothes for the kids, petrol – and come up with a figure. And they'll be shocked and horrified: "I can't ask for that, he'll be furious!"

'I want to shake them. They're getting *divorced*! Why are they still putting his needs ahead of their own?'

Show me the money

In the divorce game, as in life, information is power. You need to know what financial cards are in play if you want to come out of this well.

'You'd be astonished how many women have no idea what their husbands earn, or how much they're worth,' says Carina. 'And once he's left the house, it's like getting blood out of a stone trying to find out.

'When I found out my husband was having an affair, I wanted to throw him out of the house straight away, but I knew I'd end up with nothing. He was a very smart businessman, and good at keeping things out of reach of the taxman. If he thought I wanted a divorce, he'd have made sure I never got a penny.

'So every day I waved him off to the office with a smile on my face, then ransacked his study. I went through his computer, his files, everything, taking care to make sure he never knew I'd been there.

'I was shocked at what I found. He'd been shifting money to an offshore account in Guernsey for more than a year. He'd liquidated our joint stock portfolio, and used the cash to buy a flat in Fulham in his name.

'He'd also got a huge bonus for the previous year, which he hadn't told me about, and agreed a stock option with his firm, which meant his salary on paper was about half its real worth.

'I hired a lawyer, and gave her copies of everything. When he walked out on me without a word of explanation nine months later, he took all the paperwork with him, thinking I'd be screwed. His lawyer offered me a pathetic lump sum and virtually no maintenance, claiming he was almost broke because of the recession.

'When we produced the hard evidence that he was lying, their case collapsed like a limp balloon. I ended up keeping the house, plus a share of his pension and maintenance until the children turn eighteen. If I hadn't done my homework, I'd have got nothing. He'd have seen me on the street rather than share.'

Lindsay, 44, housewife

'Legally, both parties are obliged to declare their assets and income, but in practice, men often lie. They salt money away in offshore accounts, take chunks of their income in stock options, or simply refuse to provide the documentation we request. It's hard for a judge to make a fair ruling when we can't prove what a man is actually worth. "Knowing" he's got funds stashed away in Jersey isn't the same as putting the bank statement on the table.

'I always tell my clients that if the marriage hasn't blown up yet, and you have enough time, get as much paperwork together as you can. You're not doing anything underhand. You're entitled to know the facts. The more information we have, the stronger our bargaining position.'

Gather your evidence. Take copies of every financial statement, bank account, tax return, salary slip, credit-card statement, pension-fund advice and property deed that you can find. Go back at least twelve months. Apply the skills we discussed in Chapter Four: Snoop on the Dog, and turn over every stone until you've got what you need.

What's yours is mine

The courts will consider two principle factors when determining the division of assets and/or maintenance and child-support payments.

First, they'll look at what's available: his income, your income (or potential income) and your joint assets, including property, cash, shares and pensions.

If you have children, the chances are good that you'll be able to keep the matrimonial home, plus most of the contents apart from his personal items, *as long as* he can still afford to buy or rent a small place of his own. If you want to own it outright, rather than have him simply keep paying the mortgage, you may have to pay him a lump sum from other assets to balance things out, but a court won't want to uproot the kids from what's familiar at such a difficult time in their lives unless there's really no other option.

The reality is that unless you're a prostitute on crack, children still usually end up staying with their mother, particularly if they're young (though if they're teenagers, you may well fight *not* to have them). He'll be liable for child support until they're either seventeen or have completed full-time education.

His maintenance to you, on the other hand, will depend on whether you work and, if so, how great the disparity in your earnings is.

Since most women are the primary childcarers, our incomes inevitably suffer as we give up work, or step from the fast track into the slow-mo lane of part-time work and the school run. In most cases, therefore, the court will be looking at how much *he* has to give *you*, rather than the other way around.

It's not pleasant to be financially dependent on someone who doesn't give a toss about you any more. But it could be some time before you can stand on your own two feet, whereas your husband's ability to earn his own living is entirely unaffected by his marital status.

Don't feel guilty or beholden. Be in no doubt: *you've earned every penny.*

Money-laundering

Having established your joint marital worth, the court will then look at both your needs and his. (You may think he deserves to live in a skip near the railway station, but sadly a court will think otherwise.)

These include obvious big-ticket expenses, such as the mortgage and gas bill, but the list goes right down the food chain to haircuts, window cleaners and presents for your children's friends' birthday parties. You only get one shot at this: make sure you're thorough and accurate (I'm giving you a list below to get you started, but you'll probably find plenty more that pertain to your individual circumstances).

Don't over-egg the pudding and exaggerate – but don't sell yourself short either. And remember, you will have to prove these expenses, including the supermarket shop, so *keep receipts.*

The law is a great believer in the status quo. This means that whatever your situation and standard of living at the time of your break-up, it becomes the gold standard by which everything else is going to be judged. If you have the heart-wrenching luxury of knowing in advance that divorce is not far around the corner, you can at least use it to your advantage.

'I'd never advise a client to suddenly go out and act like she's just won the lottery,' says Carina Matthews, 'but there's no getting away from the fact that if you can skew your regular expenses upwards in the months before a divorce, it's easier for me to argue that your needs and accustomed standard of living should be pegged higher.

'Put it this way: now is *not* the time for a wife to cut back.'

If your children are at private schools, or you plan for them to be, organize a school fees payment plan now. If your marital funds run to it, set aside a lump sum; otherwise start paying the appropriate monthly amounts into a suitable plan. This, it goes without saying, should be from your joint account.

Once you've established this sort of precedent, a court will usually order a father to keep up the payments after you separate. It will certainly prevent him from claiming that you had always intended little David to attend the local sink comprehensive, so that he can spend the school fees on a fortnight in the Maldives with the Bitch instead.

Next, think about your car. If he's got a brand-new top-of-the-range BMW and you're still trundling to Sainsbury's in an eight-year-old hatchback, now is the time to suggest you trade up.

(Bribe the local garage mechanic to have it fail its MoT if you have to. You probably won't have to resort to giving him a quick blow-job in the pit; the sheer novelty of the request for it to *fail* should probably be incentive enough.)

When you split, you usually each get to keep your own car, so make sure yours is going to last you through the next few years. The money you spend together during the lifetime of your marriage is usually written off, to all intents and purposes. Remember, it could be quite a while before you have the kind of disposable income to buy these things once you're managing on his maintenance cheques, so get your house in order now.

A laundry list to get you started

Mortgage/rent

Council tax

Household insurance

Health insurance

Service charges

Electricity

Gas

Water

Food

Pension contributions

Dentist

School fees

Nanny/au pair

Car payments

Car insurance

Road tax

Car service/MoT

Parking permit/
congestion charge

Petrol

Phone/cable/internet

Mobile phone

TV licence

Window cleaner

Medicines

Pocket money
for the kids

Haircuts

Museums and
school trips

Meals out

French/piano etc. tutors

Brownies/Scouts/sports
subs

Pony Club

School uniform

Clothes

Household goods (light
bulbs etc.)

Holidays

Children's parties

Christmas and
birthday gifts

Books/DVDs

Cinema

Gym subscription

Grooming (leg wax,
facial, etc.)

Dry-cleaning

Toiletries

Newspapers/magazines

Stationery/stamps

School supplies

Therapist

Obviously going out and blowing half a million on silk wallpaper isn't a good idea – if you take the piss, a judge may deduct your decorating bill from your share of the cash – but you'll usually get away with upgrading certain items around the house that you might 'reasonably' contend you were going to do anyway. Now is the time to buy the new sofa or all-singing, all-dancing steam washer and dryer you've always wanted.

If you've been talking about adding a conservatory or finishing off the attic, do it now. You can't unring the bell; courts take a very 'what's done is done' approach to marital expenses.

If you aren't currently working, now is *not* the time to get a job. Again, once you've set a precedent, it's hard to backtrack, and his maintenance to you will take your income into account. You may want to spend more time with your children to help them through all of this, and you don't want to be trapped as a working mother if that's the case.

You can always go back to work once the dust from the divorce has settled. Assuming you're young enough, a court may allow for your 'potential' earnings, but it's hard to quantify, particularly if you haven't worked for several years because of the children, and they'll err on the lower side if there are no actual figures available to consider.

Remember: if he wishes, he may appeal for your maintenance and/or child support payments to be reduced if your circumstances – or his – change at any time. Similarly, you may go back to court to request an increase. (This is one of the reasons a 'clean break settlement' – which applies *only* to maintenance and/or the division of capital assets, and not child support, and *cannot* be varied once agreed – is often sought.)

Don't let him start economizing now, either. Keep on having smoked salmon for breakfast if that's what you've always done (and if you haven't, now would be the time to start). He's as aware of the standard-of-living touchstone as you are, and if he suddenly wants to dump the cleaner and sack the au pair, you don't have to be a genius to figure out the reason. It'll be much harder for him to argue that a nanny is a needless extravagance if you've had one for the last four years.

Quietly set aside enough cash for an emergency fighting fund. You need to have enough money to last you a minimum of three months; if and when the split does happen, he may – particularly if there's another woman egging him on – start fighting dirty and simply not pay you.

Rest assured, a court can and will order him to make interim maintenance payments pending a final financial deal between you, but this can take time, and in the meantime you have children to feed and a lawyer to pay – they'll require a retainer, usually around £1,000: expensive, but this is one time you can't afford to skimp.

If you don't work and have no funds of your own, open an account at a different bank from your usual one. Cash cheques from your joint account – not enough to cause comment if he checks your statements; if he does ask, tell him it was for repairs to that rust-bucket of a car you really *must* replace soon, darling – and then pay the cash into your private account.

Over a period of a few months you can set aside enough to last you in case of emergency; and hey, if by some miracle you do stay together, it'll pay for that celebratory red dress you've been eyeing up in that gorgeous boutique down the road.

The mills of justice

Once the divorce is under way, it will take every ounce of strength and guts you have to hold it together. I'm not going to pretend otherwise: it will be the most bitter, painful and gruelling experience you'll ever have.

Your life will be brutally stripped bare. In the blizzard of paperwork your lawyers exchange with his, you will learn far too much about his life, too, and every fresh detail – the bank statements that reveal his affair started while you were still pregnant with your youngest child; the credit-card bill detailing their recent trip to Rome, the one place he always promised to take you and never did; his appeal to have maintenance reduced because, oh God, she's pregnant – will flay you alive.

You'll think you're inured to the shock, and then something will happen to take your breath away, some fresh indignity will be heaped upon you, and you'll be plunged into deepest despair once again.

Meanwhile, the legal fees will pile up. The onslaught is relentless. The most intimate, personal information will be debated publicly by lawyers who've never even met you.

There will be times you'd agree to anything, sign anything, to make it stop.

Hold fast. I know how hard it is, but you *will* come through it. The mills of justice grind slow, but they grind exceedingly small. The endless forms and affidavits and court dates *will* come to an end, and you *will* be free of it all.

Keep your chin up. Have a good cry, take a nice hot bath with a cool glass of wine, and start again tomorrow.

In a nutshell

- Diamonds really are a girl's best friend . . . but hard evidence comes a close second
- Do your homework, and find the dirt
- Play to win: remember, nice girls finish last
- Never agree to anything without a lawyer
- Only those with money have the luxury of thinking it doesn't matter. Fight for what's yours
- Conduct your own one-woman economic stimulus plan. Spend, darling!
- Do buy a new car/build an extension/book a second holiday
- Don't get a job
- Stick with it. You will survive and flourish in the end

Remember: there's no such thing as an amicable divorce!

Chapter Thirteen
Revenge is a Dish Best Served Now

The New Testament tells us to turn the other cheek, but give me an Old Testament eye-for-an-eye any time. Sometimes you just want to get the bastard's balls in a vice and squeeze until they go pop.

It was Byron who wrote, in *Don Juan*, the story of the archetypal love-'em-and-leave-'em swaggerer: 'Sweet is revenge – especially to women.'

Like poison, revenge is generally thought of as a female weapon, even though it's also occasionally wielded by men. But while male retaliation tends to be of the immediate, run-him-through variety, women sit and stew. And plot. And plan.

The anthropological explanation is that since women can't confront men physically, they have no choice but to devise stratagems to get their own back. When a man walks out on his wife for a Bitch with big tits, there's not much a woman can do except cross him off her Christmas-card list. And buy diamonds.

When all else is lost, and saving your marriage is no longer an option, there's nothing like seizing back control in a beautifully crafted moment of retribution to restore your self-esteem.

Enough of divorce, and the rational, sensible, grown-up options. Let's hear it for the girls who got their own back in ways most of us only dream about.

Some paybacks are so spectacular they pass into legend.

The severed parts

On the night of 23 June 1993, John Wayne Bobbitt arrived at his home in Virginia, drunk after a night of partying, and went to bed. His wife Lorena, who was clearly feeling a bit narky, got up, went into the kitchen, picked up a carving knife and returned to the bedroom, where her husband was already asleep and no doubt snoring his damn head off. So she cut off his penis, as you do.

She then left the apartment, with the penis, and went for a drive. Passing through some fields, she stopped, rolled down the window and lobbed his willy through it.

All of the above makes perfect sense. Less understandable is that she then called the emergency services and helped them find the severed member, so they were able to pack it in ice and sew it back on. Shame on you, Lorena.

But still. Despite her regrettable fit of remorse, Lorena remains a feminist icon (the kind who has quizzes named after her). Even the jury acquitted her when they heard how her husband had been catting around. All hail Lorena.

In a bizarre twist, John Wayne subsequently formed a

band called The Severed Parts. Unsurprisingly, it was something of a flop (if you'll excuse the pun).

Fly me to the Graham-Moon

Closer to home, Lady Sarah Graham-Moon hit the headlines in 1992 when she sought vengeance for her husband's dalliance with a blonde Berkshire neighbour.

Initially determined to keep their split amicable (all together now: *There's no such thing as an amicable divorce!*), she lost the plot when she spotted her husband's prized blue BMW parked in her younger rival's driveway, and promptly emptied five litres of white gloss all over it.

That was just the beginning. The furious aristocrat returned home and chopped the sleeves off three of her husband's cashmere coats and thirty-two of his bespoke suits, before distributing the contents of his wine cellar throughout the village on their neighbours' doorsteps.

At the time, Sir Peter Graham-Moon estimated her wrecking spree cost him £35,000.

'It gave me a hell of a buzz,' Lady Graham-Moon allegedly said later.

A recent study by researchers at University College, London, discovered that volunteers registered a surge of activity in the reward centre of their brains when actors who had cheated in a monetary investment game were given simulated electric shocks. In contrast, when 'fair' players were given shocks, the volunteers showed increased activity in the pain-related parts of their brain.

So there you have it: revenge really *is* sweet.

Bespoke vengeance

I once briefly dated an advertising executive, the kind of man who had white suede sofas and no books in the house – 'too messy, and the spines don't match'.

It didn't take long for me to work out that the relationship wasn't going anywhere, but just as I sat him down to break the news, he pre-empted me with his own Dear Jane speech – on the grounds that I was a natural blonde. Yes, I kid you not. 'Mocha', apparently, 'went better with the sheets'.

Outraged that I had been deleted merely because my pubic hair didn't complement his linen, I went through all the red-top Sunday supplements that weekend, carefully cutting out order forms for mattresses, encyclopaedias, stair-lifts, porcelain figurines – anything he'd consider hideously bad taste. Then I ordered everything to his address, cash on delivery.

It didn't do him any bodily harm, but the aggravation factor was sky high. I heard from mutual friends that he was boxing up return packages in his ex-minimalist apartment for weeks, and cursing me all the while.

And that's the key to the unique satisfaction revenge affords. It ensures you're not forgotten; and it can be tailor-made to suit the peculiar idiosyncracies of its victim.

It's easy enough to key your ex's car, or spray-paint graffiti on his garden wall. Satisfying, no doubt, but not really very clever.

We've all heard the apocryphal stories of the girl who called Australia from her boyfriend's phone and left the receiver off the hook when he was on holiday for two weeks; or the woman who sewed prawns into her ex's curtain hems, forcing him eventually to move house because of the unidentifiable stink – and *take the curtains with him.*

There are the wives who get hold of their cheating husband's phone bill, call up every number on it that they don't recognize and, pretending to be a health officer, tell the person on the other end of the line that their man has contracted a sexually transmitted disease and they needed to get to a VD clinic a.s.a.p.

An entire cult business has sprung up around 'jilt ads', such as the following billboard that appeared recently in the US:

Hi Dan,
   Do I have your attention now?
   I know all about her, you dirty, sneaky, immoral, unfaithful, poorly endowed slimeball. Everything's caught on tape.
   Your (soon-to-be-ex) wife,
   Karyn
   PS I paid for this billboard from OUR joint bank account.

But my favourite stories of revenge are those carefully and wittily designed to cause the maximum irritation with the minimum of effort and expense.

A girlfriend of mine was married to a literary man, who she discovered had been cheating on her. He owned some 5,000 weighty tomes in dusty book jackets, filling shelves from floor to ceiling throughout their house. Just before she left, his wife switched all the jackets around and even now, five years later, he'll reach for *A History of Witchcraft* and find himself holding *Butler's Lives of the Saints*.

I feel for him, I really do – it's just that it was so neat, so *beautifully* tailored to drive him, and *only* him, potty. In the annals of revenge stories, it may seem lame. But in point of fact, nothing could have pissed him off more. It takes a woman's touch to know how to bring a man down.

One newly-ex-boyfriend's parting shot to another friend was the regretful admission that he'd miss her delicious cooking more than anything else. Incensed, she hand-delivered his favourite indulgence to him: her speciality, a moist and rich chocolate lava cake.

Through the letterbox. Ingredient by ingredient.

The best revenge is living well

Revenge can be satisfying and therapeutic, but it can also cost you dear, financially and emotionally. To quote Francis Bacon, 'A man who contemplates revenge keeps his wounds green.'

Vengeance has been likened to biting a dog because the dog bit you. Leave it to the Bard to put it best: 'Heat not a furnace for your foe so hot that it do singe yourself.'

In the end, revenge won't change the circumstances that brought you such grief. Lorena Bobbitt's entire life became defined by her husband's penis – surely the very fate she wanted to avoid. Lady Graham-Moon's moment of vengeance has followed her around for nearly twenty years, and certainly compromised her divorce settlement.

It's hard to be free of the past if you tie it like a millstone about your neck.

Ultimately, as the saying has it, the best revenge is living well. Eleanor Roosevelt was once described as getting even with her enemies in a way that was 'almost cruel. She forgave them.'

Sinatra put it best: 'The best revenge is massive success.'

Slice his suits in two if you must. But once you've satisfied your need to see him get his come-uppance, let it go. Move on with your own life. The sweetest revenge against the Bitch is to be happy again. After all, *she's* the one stuck with a louse who has a proven track record of infidelity, not you.

Two years after my husband and I parted, I met the man who became my second husband. These days, I'm kissed awake by a six-foot-five, blue-eyed, blond American philosopher who's more than twenty years younger than my first husband and a trained chef to boot.

And in the end my ex's adultery was a brilliant career move on my part. It's given me a USP of sorts. After our divorce, my rather wicked novel *The Adultery Club* shot straight into the top-ten bestseller list. Hey, if life gives you lemons, make lemonade.

Recently, the editor of a well-known glossy magazine rang me and opened the conversation with the line 'I really need to talk to you about our cover story. I hear you're the expert on infidelity.'

Go, Sinatra.

In a nutshell

'Don't get mad, get even'
– Robert F. Kennedy

'Revenge has no more quenching effect on emotions than salt water has on thirst' – Walter Weckler

'Surviving well is your finest revenge' – Morgan Nito

Chapter Fourteen
Interviews With the Infidels

I know. You don't want to give the bastards airtime. This fight is between you and the Bitch. But remember what we said right back at the beginning in Chapter Two?

Know thy enemy.

A lot of the excuses Infidels come up with to explain why they can't keep their trousers zipped are so much Grade A bullshit. But now and again they accidentally tell an important truth (remember: if a roomful of chimps were stuck in front of typewriters and left to hit keys at random for a few millennia, eventually they'd come up with *War and Peace*).

Men *will* cheat if you take your eye off the ball and put your kids at the centre of the relationship. They *will* find another woman to have sex with if you won't. They need you to pay attention to them; even if the sex isn't great between you, a little affection goes a long way. Constant criticism will grind a man down to the point where he'll have an affair out of desperation.

And of course some men will have an affair no matter *what* you do.

So first, here's the story of a man named Brady, who was bringing up three very lovely girls . . .

Man of the house

Brady Perry, aged forty-nine, is a politician. He's been married to his wife, Gillian, a stay-at-home mother of three, for twenty-eight years. They live in London and have a daughter aged twenty-seven, and twin girls of twenty-five.

My father walked out on me and my mother when I was nine. My mother did her best, but she wasn't one of life's copers. She relied on me a lot to do things my dad had done, like mow the lawn, but she also gave me far too much responsibility for my age.

She let me make major decisions, like what car to buy or whether we should move house. I don't mean she asked my opinion; she actually left it up to me.

We'd go out for dinner to smart restaurants, and she'd tell me to wear a pinstriped suit she'd bought, and I'd have to sit across from her and talk about current events and politics. She made me stay up and watch *Newsnight* so I'd be good company for her. Other kids read *Spiderman* comics; I had to read *The Times*.

Then, when I was thirteen, she met Kevin. He owned a local taxi-hire company, and was fat and boring, but he worshipped the ground she walked on, and she lapped it up. She sent me off to boarding school as soon as they got married.

I spent the next five years bloody miserable. I was bullied because I came across as a weird little mini-adult, thanks to my mother. I didn't know how to be a teenager. I hated her for choosing Kevin over me and sending me away.

When I left school, I went to St Andrews to study politics, and met Gillian in my first year. She was studying Chinese and her dream was to be a translator at the UN. She was bright and confident and attractive. We lost our virginity to each other, and as soon as we graduated I asked her to marry me. Looking back, I think I was desperate for a family.

We hadn't planned to have kids quite so soon, but Sarah was born less than a year later, when we were both twenty-two. Gillian was just starting to think about getting her career back on track when our twin girls were born eighteen months after Sarah.

Having three babies in nappies was hard work, especially for Gillian. I was just starting out in politics and we didn't have much money, so we couldn't afford any help. My mother was wrapped up in Kevin, so she wasn't a hands-on grandmother. If it hadn't been for Gillian's mother, I don't know how we'd have survived those first few years. The only time we got out of the house was when she babysat.

I know it's unfair, but I found coming home to Gillian and the girls boring. As soon as I walked through the door, she'd practically throw the kids at me. She'd yell, 'I've been stuck in the house all day with the three of them! Now it's your turn!' and burst into tears.

She'd always been so intelligent and interesting, but now she had nothing to say. Her only topics of conversation were pottytraining and when to put the twins on solids.

She let her appearance go, too. The baby weight stayed, and she stopped bothering to get her hair done or wear make-up when we went out. I'd try to encourage her to buy pretty clothes, but she said there was no point when the kids would just throw up on them. She practically lived in jeans and T-shirts.

Our sex life went into the crapper. We had sex about once a month, if that, and it was dull and perfunctory. I could practically see Gillian calculating how much time she had to sleep before the twins woke up.

As my career took off, I needed a wife by my side who was an asset. Someone who could sparkle and entertain and charm the right people. But Gillian refused even to come to work functions, saying she was too tired, or couldn't be bothered. I tried not to blame her, but I resented the fact that she always put the kids' needs first.

I didn't consciously decide to have an affair, but I didn't put up a fight, either. Melissa worked in the press office, and reminded me very much of how Gillian used to be. She was tough and savvy, and made it plain that if I was interested, she was very much available.

I told her I had no intention of leaving Gillian. I still loved my wife, and adored the girls. It wasn't really Gillian's fault she'd been overwhelmed by having so many kids so young. And of course I had my career to think about.

Our affair lasted about a year. Eventually Melissa met someone she wanted to get serious about, so we ended things, with no hard feelings on either side.

Since then, I've had about six relationships outside my marriage, lasting from about six months to four years. I'm not into one-night stands or flings. I'm a one-woman man. I've always been very careful to make it clear that the affairs could never lead to anything permanent. If I feel a girl is getting too serious, I extricate myself before anyone gets hurt.

I don't think of myself as a philanderer. It's not about the chase or the thrill for me. I just need more in the way of physical and emotional closeness than my wife can give me.

There was only one woman I was tempted to leave Gillian for. Jo was intelligent, funny, and really dirty in bed. She had a son of her own, and didn't want any more kids, so she'd have been perfect for me. But in the end I couldn't do it. It wouldn't have been fair on Gillian, and the scandal would have put paid to my career.

Jo said once that I used women, as a way of getting back at my mother. I don't think that's true. I love women.

Gillian would be devastated if she knew I'd been unfaithful to her. But I'd never leave my wife. I have a huge amount of respect for the way she looks after our family and is bringing up the girls.

Maybe one day when I'm too old, or women don't find me attractive, I'll be faithful. I'm sure there will come a day not too far off when I'll slink home with my tail between my legs.

A death sentence

Christopher Silver, aged forty-four, lives in Manchester and is an independent financial adviser. He's been married to Charlotte, who is thirty-eight and has MS, for twelve years. They have no children.

My wife's had MS for the past nine years. In that time, I've seen her go from a sexy, vivacious woman to a wheelchair-bound cripple. I've never stopped loving her, but there are times I almost hate her too.

I know it's a thousand times worse for her, but she's not the only one who's suffering. This disease didn't just rob her of her life; it took the life I'd planned away from me too. I feel lonely, helpless, and trapped – it would be selfish and cruel to leave her, but why do I have to give up any hope of a life too? I've always wanted children, but she'll never be able to give me a baby.

I promised to love her in sickness and in health, but how many of us who make that vow ever really expect to have to follow through? She was only twenty-nine when she was diagnosed. Ever since, we've both lived under a death sentence.

It's not as if my wife has made up for her physical disabilities by being a partner to me in other ways. She's very demanding and complains endlessly, but never thinks to ask how I feel. It's as if her disease must come first, all the time.

I try not to judge her too harshly, but she's not the woman I thought she was. I have experience of disability. My sister was born with one leg, but she's never let that stop her. She runs and sails and does everything her friends do. She's never felt sorry for herself. My wife drowns in self-pity. I guess it's true that adversity brings out the best and worst in people.

About two years ago, I met Louise. To begin with, it was just such a relief to have someone I could be myself with; someone I could lean on, instead of always having to be 'the rock'. She gives me the strength to go home and deal with my wife's illness day after day, night after night. If it wasn't for her, I would have left by now.

Some people assume my wife and I have an 'understanding' about sex, since we can't sleep together, but that's never been further from the truth. She often breaks down in tears and accuses me of being unfaithful, and reminds me of my promise to her when we married. She even gets upset if I bring porn into the house and look after myself in the bathroom. She says she's had to sacrifice a sex life, and if I loved her I wouldn't think about it.

I'm so sick of living a lie. Sometimes I think about telling my wife, and bringing it all out into the open, but I'm afraid she'd do something stupid. She's already threatened to kill herself if I left. If she'd accept that Louise meets certain needs, I'd stay with her until the end.

Three months ago, Louise told me she was expecting our baby. It's the best thing that's ever happened to me, but now I feel even more torn than I did before. I know this mess is of my own making, but can you really blame me?

I'm not a bad person. I just want to feel loved, to come home to a wife and family, to have someone care about how my day went. Is that really so wrong?

The seventh commandment

Dennis Coppard, aged forty-four, is the CEO of an IT company. He is married to Laura, his second wife, who is forty-one, and lives in London. He has three children, now twelve, eleven and eight, by his first wife, Annabel.

It genuinely didn't occur to me until I was walking up the aisle on my wedding day that sleeping with my mistress was about to be elevated from a trifling misdemeanour to breaking one of the Ten Commandments.

That's serious stuff. Suddenly I couldn't tear my eyes away from the tablets on the church wall. Number seven seemed written in words of fire: 'Thou shalt not commit adultery.' It's so bloody proscriptive. Not much room for a loophole there.

But I've never been very religious. I was fond of Annabel, my bride, but I didn't fancy her in the slightest – awful legs – and never had any intention of being faithful to her.

My mistress, Bella, was a fantastic fuck. Really dirty in bed. After an afternoon with her, I could barely walk.

Annabel had no interest in sex. She'd put out occasionally in the early days, but once we got engaged she unilaterally decided sex was off limits until our wedding night. By the time we got to the church, I hadn't had sex with her in six months. What did she think I was, a monk?

I'd been seeing Bella for about six months before I met Annabel, but there was never any question of marrying her. She was too young, too nervy, and a bit mad. I kept telling her I'd never marry her, and she kept insisting she'd change my mind. Even after I married Annabel, she still thought I'd marry her. I was bloody careful about contraception, I can tell you. The last thing I needed was Bella turning up on my doorstep with a happy bundle.

Annabel, on the other hand, had 'perfect mother' written all over her. She was well connected and used to mixing in the same social circles as me. She could host a dinner party and hit it off with other wives. I really wanted kids, and she seemed to fit the bill.

Our sex life was pretty dismal. We had three kids in five years, so I suppose we must have fucked three times. I'm damned if it was any more.

If she'd agreed to sex every morning maybe it would have helped – but there are still the afternoons to fill.

I need sex every day. I'm not going to apologize for that. She knew that going into our marriage. You'd have thought she'd have realized that if she didn't have sex with me, I'd have it with someone else.

I assumed she understood the rules. I'd never leave her or the kids, but she had to accept I'd keep a mistress. It's not as if she wanted to have sex with me herself. I really don't see the harm in getting it elsewhere. If your husband loved skiing and you didn't, would you mind if he skied with his friends while you went shopping? What difference would it make to you?

Bella was my regular mistress for about three years, although of course I had plenty of other short flings too. Then she started turning into a bit of a bunny boiler, ringing home at three in the morning and so on. I ended it. She went off and married someone else, though we still meet up for the occasional fuck. I'm only human.

Then I met a really fucking sexy woman about ten years older than me. Maddie was amazing; there was literally nothing off limits. I had a fling with her daughter, too, though not both of them at the same time. I do have limits.

Eventually, Annabel found out about Maddie – I was bloody unlucky: a friend of hers spotted us in a restaurant in New York – and she went off the deep end. Completely overreacted: threw me out of the house, forbade Maddie from ever meeting the children, rang my parents and screamed at them down the phone. A week later, she came round to my hotel room and begged me to take her back. Put on this black lace basque and stockings under her raincoat – it wasn't sexy, it was embarrassing. Like seeing your mother in fishnets.

Maddie and I were an item for about two years after my divorce, but she was never going to be a permanent fixture. Her choice, not mine. She liked her independence, and she didn't want the family baggage that came with my three kids. Plus, she said I'd never manage to be faithful to any woman, and she didn't want to be the wife sitting at home wondering where I was. Smart woman, Maddie.

I do quite like being married, though. I like the companionship of having someone around, and the convenience of a fuck every morning. A lot of social events need a wife. Maddie was great in bed, but not particularly attractive, and if I'm honest she was a bit common. She never quite fitted in.

So about four years ago, I decided to take the plunge again. I was more careful this time; I made certain Laura knew the rules. We had a conversation early on. She'd never ask any questions, and I'd never fuck any of her friends. She didn't want to be embarrassed.

Laura is smart, sexy and funny as hell. She lets me have sex every couple of days, and doesn't ask what I get up to when she's away on business.

My current mistress is a dynamic blonde with huge tits who gives the best blow-jobs I've ever had. She's Catholic, which explains it. As far as I'm aware, Laura doesn't know. I think she'd be OK with it, but there's no need to push it. I don't want another expensive divorce.

If Laura had been my first wife and the mother of my kids, maybe I'd have been faithful to her. The thing is, I've been getting away with affairs for too long now. I don't think I could change if I wanted to.

Chapter Fifteen
Ten Things Men Really Hate About Women

1. Diets

'I can't stand women who bitch about their weight all the time and count every calorie. Who gives a fuck about a few curves? As long as she's not bursting out all over, we don't care. I want a woman with passion for food, for sex, for life.'   *Ed, 27, trainee accountant*

2. Girl-women

'I hate babyish women who do all that girly talk and twist their hair round their little fingers and do the Shy Di thing with their fringe. It's kind of sick. What am I, a kiddy fiddler?'   *Bryan, 30, sales manager*

3. Controlling women

'Women who take control of everything, and say things like "If you want a job doing well, do it yourself," and then bitch they never get any help and have to do all the work. Women are their own worst enemy.'   *Ted, 36, nurse*

4. Duty fucks

'Girls who act like they're doing you a huge favour by sleeping with you. A duty fuck. It makes me bitter and pissed off. It's like, you open your legs and I'm expected to kiss your ass with gratitude. You're not keeper of the only cunt in the world.'   *Nick, 31, car salesman*

5. Bitchy women

'I hate it when women bitch about each other. They'll be really nice to a girl's face, and the second they're out of earshot, it's all, "Did you see her *thighs*? She's put on so much weight!" What am I supposed to do with that?'

Mitchell, 24, student

6. Hypocrites

'It drives me crazy when women wear really revealing clothing, low-cut tops and short skirts, and then get angry with men for looking at them as sexual objects. If you don't want me to talk to your tits, don't shove them in my face.'

Dave, 28, doorman

7. Unromantic women

'Women who complain that men aren't romantic, but then never do anything romantic themselves. They sit there and expect men to do all the running: give them flowers, buy them jewellery, whisk them off to Paris for the weekend. But what do *they* do? Men want to be romanced too, you know.'   *Jude, 33, salesman*

8. Ladettes

'Girls who drink too much. In my line of work, I see it all the time, and it's really ugly. They swear and belch and smoke and flash their arses like men, and then wonder why they don't get treated like women. I hate this whole ladette culture. I don't know a single man who doesn't.'

Red, 26, DJ

9. Passivity in bed

'Women who're lazy in the sack. The kind who just lie there and think of England. Too many women lack creativity and imagination in bed. They're always telling you what they *don't* want. They'll say no to something new without even trying it.'   *Mark, 29, IT consultant*

10. Women who take advantage

'I'm fed up with being taken advantage of by women. They expect you to forgive their aggression and bad temper and Christ knows what else because of their "hormones". But woe betide any *man* who has a bad day! They want us to change tyres and put up shelves, but to treat them as equals. We're expected to bring home the bacon, then cook dinner and change nappies when we get there. And what are *women* bringing to the table? Nothing but more complaints.'   *Paul, 42, substance-abuse therapist*

Chapter Sixteen

You Don't Want to Hear This, But . . .

What would you give to be able to turn the clock back?

I don't think there's a person alive who hasn't wanted to step back in time, if only for five minutes. Think of the heartache you could spare yourself if you could warn your younger incarnation to do things differently. (There'd be no disastrous bubble perms or leg warmers in my photo album, for a start. Thank God Facebook didn't exist in the eighties or I'd never have lived it down.)

Imagine if he'd never parked his car outside your sister's flat at midnight when he was supposed to be away in Manchester on business. If his mistress hadn't thrown her lipsticked cigarette butt in your toilet bowl for you to find; or received flowers on a credit card you didn't even know he had.

Imagine if he'd never had that affair at all.

I truly wish I could send you spinning back in time. Maybe then you'd understand that my 'Karma Chameleon' phase was *not my fault*. And perhaps you'd even nudge your life on to a different track, one that didn't ever include the Bitch.

I can't do that for you; if only.

But perhaps I can give you the next best thing: a second chance.

For your relationship to work, it must now change. An affair is a terrible way for this to happen, but perhaps it can be the catalyst you both need to rediscover each other and fall in love again.

It won't happen overnight. Trust takes a long time to rebuild. But if the two of you decide you want to make it happen, you must let go of your anger and resentment. You won't ever forget, but you need to learn to forgive. That doesn't mean giving him *carte blanche* to turn the page and pretend it never happened. It means deciding that the future is more important than the past.

It also means accepting that *your* behaviour needs to change, as well as his. That's what this chapter is about.

And for those of you to whom the worst has not yet happened, whose husbands and lovers and boyfriends haven't strayed, yet, though perhaps they are already thinking about it, already starting to stay out late and confide in someone other than you; for those of you reading this book *just in case* (and I truly, madly, deeply hope most of you fall into this happier category), then perhaps this chapter is the most important of all.

This is the chapter that could just save your relationship.

You may not like what I'm about to tell you. You may have already muttered indignantly when you read Chapter Nine and I told you that yes, you *do* have to 'play games' if you want to keep your man all to yourself. In that case, you're going to be *seriously* pissed off by the time you finish this one.

But frankly, I'm tired of women who flip out when you suggest that the path to a happy marriage will involve you doing things to – horrors! – *please your man.*

Why should I dress up in bloody suspenders and high heels when he doesn't give a damn about his appearance? they demand. *Why do I have to run around trying to please him? This isn't the fifties! Why do I have to be the one to make this marriage work?*

I'll tell you why. Because whether your marriage stands or fails depends on *you.*

A good man is hard to find, not keep. Once you've kissed enough toads and found your handsome prince, all you need to do is show him affection, respect, love and approval. If you give him these, *he will not stray.*

Bitter truth

When you married, you promised to have and to hold this man for better or for worse, for richer, for poorer, in sickness and in health, to love and to cherish, until death did you part (or words to that effect). Did you include a clause in there that said 'only if he's really nice to me first'? 'Fraid not.

Even if you're not married, you presumably love this man, right? Which means that showing him a little respect and affection is hardly throwing the feminist movement under a bus.

> 'Love is always patient and kind; it is never jealous; love is never boastful or conceited; it is never rude or selfish; it does not take offence, and is not resentful. Love takes no pleasure in other people's sins but delights in the truth; it is always ready to excuse, to trust, to hope, and to endure whatever comes. Love does not come to an end.'
>
> *1 Corinthians 13: 4–8 (Jerusalem Bible)*

To paraphrase that great ladies' man, JFK: too many women get married thinking about what their marriage and their man can do for them, and not what they can do for their marriage.

If you're not prepared to *give* as well as take, your marriage will crash and burn. It's as simple as that.

The truth is that the more you love a man, the more you cherish and respect him, the more he'll love and cherish and respect you back.

Remember: I'm talking about a fundamentally decent man here. If you've wilfully married a Philanderer – and don't give me any bullshit about not knowing he was a cheating bastard: you *knew* he was a bad boy when you took him on. You just thought you could change him, and now you're in a strop because you can't – then all bets are off. But *a good man* won't look elsewhere unless you drive him to it.

Oh, it's a bitter truth, isn't it? I can feel your hackles rising already. *Things may not have been perfect at home, but that didn't mean he had to go off and shag his bloody secretary, did it? How is it* my *fault because he couldn't keep it in his trousers? Why* am *I to blame because he was so fucking weak?*

Shopaholic does divorce

Yep. I've been there. It took me more time than I care to admit to accept that I was at least partly responsible for the collapse of my marriage, and by extension my husband's affair.

Of course going off and sleeping with another woman was hardly the ideal solution to our problems.

But an affair is a man's default response when he's not getting what he needs from his woman – and you know from previous chapters that I'm not just talking about sex here.

When women are unhappy at home, we shop. I have an entire unworn section of my wardrobe devoted to ridiculously expensive designer clothes from Armani to Chanel, whose labels have never even been removed. (My daughter's going to have one hell of a vintage collection to draw on in a few years' time.)

Or we throw ourselves into our children, living through and for them, which often only serves to make our marital problems worse.

We comfort-eat. We party too hard. We hit the gym. We bitch to our girlfriends. Frequently we do all the above, plus chocolate. Anything to patch over and disguise the cracks in our marriages.

Men are simpler. They just have affairs.

While I was writing this book, my husband and his wife – yes, the very same 'Bitch' who was the recipient of those long-ago telephone sweet nothings, whose existence once caused me so much grief and pain – came to see our sons, and take them skiing for the half-term break.

Ten years is a long time. A lot of water has flowed under the bridge since the halcyon days when I longed for her to spontaneously combust so I could warm my hands as she burned.

We made our peace with one another long ago, and in fact, the 'Bitch' – who is, of course, nothing of the sort – has become an unlikely friend. But perhaps not that unlikely after all: there is nothing that binds women together like a shared experience, and what could be more shared than the experience of having been married to the same man?

Geography and circumstance mean that most of our encounters are a cordial but fleeting meet-'n'-greet as the children change hands.

This time, however, was different, for they were staying just around the corner, and we all skied together. And so, for the first time I saw how she treated my ex-husband. I saw the solicitousness with which she looked out for him, the way she nurtured him with a patience I'd still struggle to find, and put him at the centre of everything.

And I realized that I had never done that. I had never put his needs first.

OK, perhaps not *never*. But certainly not enough. When he was away working, I was lonely, bored and fed up. I expected – *demanded* – that he meet the emotional bill when he came home. I didn't think about how much his job took out of him, or what I could do to support him when he came home mentally, physically and emotionally drained. I was too busy thinking about what *I* needed from *him*.

His affair was *not* my fault. I'm not an apologist for adultery. As I've said before, you can't *make* your husband screw around. But that doesn't mean your hands are entirely clean either.

Take a long, hard look at yourself. How much do *you* give? What do *you* bring to the table?

I'm not talking about washing his laundry or tidying up his house, or even caring for his children. He can always pay someone to do all of those things. What do *you* give him that no one else on Earth can?

I know you're busy. I know you're overwhelmed with juggling your job, the kids, money worries and the ironing. But what could possibly be a better investment of time and energy than your marriage?

Luck of the draw

When I married my first husband, I was barely into my twenties. My parents had been happily married for precisely nine months longer than my existence, and I always thought that they'd been incredibly lucky to have found each other.

I assumed that you either have a great marriage or you don't. The luck of the draw, right? It never occurred to me how much blood, sweat and tears they both put into creating and sustaining that 'luck'. I thought when people said marriage was hard work that they were talking about the dusting and the washing-up.

I remember my mother once saying that every morning she woke up and *decided* to be in love with my father.

My father replied that my mother might have promised to obey him, but *he'd* promised to cherish *her*. And as he pointed out, cherishing someone – protecting and loving them tenderly, with all that that entails – can be a great deal tougher than doing as you're told.

In the years since my divorce, I've often gone back to that conversation. At the time, I didn't get it. I had no concept of love as a verb, as an attitude of mind. I thought it was some existential plane of being to which one ascended without volition or effort.

I blame Hallmark, and Hollywood, and the Romantic poets, and everyone else who's ever peddled the nonsense that love is a nice warm feeling that somehow envelops you of its own accord and makes you happy.

Effortless, unconditional love exists in the context of our children. It's a primeval, instinctive survival mechanism. There's nothing selfless or altruistic about it – although it can inspire acts of extraordinary selflessness and altruism. But in essence parents are driven by their biology to nurture the survival of their own DNA. Everything else is secondary.

> 'Love is not love
> Which alters when it alteration finds,
> Or bends with the remover to remove'
> **Shakespeare, Sonnet 116**

Love for a partner is very different. It requires huge reserves of commitment and unselfishness. It demands that you start afresh every single day. That you *decide* to be in love with them every single morning.

There are times in every relationship when they irritate you just by breathing. And those are the times you have to make the effort to love them *most*.

I want it all and I want it now

In many respects, no generation in history has been quite as selfish as ours. For both men and women, the mantra of personal happiness has become king: *I have a right to a career, a happy marriage, and children. I have a right to want and have it all.*

Yes, and we also have a right to miserable children, sleepless nights worrying about the insane size of our credit-card bills, and a closer relationship with our divorce lawyer than we ever had with our spouse.

This isn't about the battle between the sexes. This is about learning to *put someone else first*. Surely that's the definition of love?

In an ideal world, both men and women would make the same effort to nurture their relationships, and yes, that's still something we should shoot for. But the fact is that men are not as good at relationships as we are. We can't blame the poor dears – they're biologically programmed to go out and conquer the world for us and bring it home to lay at our feet. They'll still do it, if we let them. And many of them don't understand why that isn't enough.

Sitting around steaming because *he's* not trying hard enough to make your marriage work isn't going to change anything. We can't control another person's actions, only our own.

The best way to effect change is to lead by example.

A dull girl

The truth is there are only so many hours in the day. We have to make decisions and prioritize. If we allow our choices to force our relationship with our man to the bottom of the pile, we've got things arse-backwards. Trust me, sooner or later he'll return the compliment.

Of course a woman should have a job and a career if she wants it. But if we choose to have a husband and children too, we have to understand that we're not free solely to pursue our own desires the way we once were. Our family's needs must now feature in our lives as much as our own.

President Obama recently coined the term 'the Spectacular Wife', to describe women like his own wife, Michelle. Women who're high-flying and ambitious, and yet willing to put their careers on hold to back their husband's ambitions, and keep the family going.

Samantha Cameron, David Cameron's wife, is another Spectacular Wife: beautiful, stylish and bright, she may have a designer job at Smythson, but it's never allowed to get in the way of her commitments to her family, or her unreserved support for her husband's career.

I'm not suggesting for a moment that you should give up your career, and substitute your hopes or your dreams for his, or that they're in any way less important. But like it or not, *you're* the fulcrum around which your entire family turns.

Stop jockeying for position, and fighting over every inch of marital territory. Try flexing that *unselfish* muscle for a change.

Your husband needs you to be his lover, his friend, the mother of his children, and his biggest fan. Wonderful if you can manage all this *and* hold down a job running the country, but recognize that, if not, you may need to make compromises, and, yes, *sacrifices*. At least in the short term.

As Hillary Clinton has proved, there's always time for the tables to turn and the Spectacular Wife to take centre stage.

Blue balls

Let's just think about sex for a moment (trust me, he is).

You already know what you should be doing in the bedroom and, more importantly, how often you should be doing it. We've been there earlier in this book.

Now, I just want you to think about that in the context of putting his physical needs ahead of yours. Because for men, sex *is* a need. Biology designed them that way. They can no more help wanting to have sex with you than you can help craving chocolate when you've got your period.

He really *will* get blue balls if you don't fuck him on a regular basis. I'm not kidding: having a hard-on that doesn't get satisfied will cause fluid to gather in his bollocks and prostate. He'll get cramps, headaches, backache and a really bloody temper. Rather like you when you have your period, in fact.

So, does this mean you should have sex with him when you don't really feel like it?

(Take a deep breath): Sometimes, yes.

Before you throw this book across the room and denounce

me for condoning marital rape, I'm obviously talking about this in the context of consent.

Nor do I mean three days after you've just given birth, or when you're barely able to get out of bed with flu.

I'm talking about sex in the usual run of things, when you simply may not be in the mood for any one of a hundred imaginative and pressing reasons. (The ironing, for instance. Or *Corrie*.)

How many things do you expect him to do for you when he doesn't feel like it? Going to work at a job he hates to support his family, for one. Spending Christmas at your parents' rather than his. Having your friends over for dinner even when he doesn't like them. Getting up early on Saturday morning to deal with the kids so you can have a lie-in.

But sex isn't the same, right?

Why not? Doing something you don't particularly feel like doing, be it painting the ceiling, or having sex, requires you to put someone else first. Think of it as a loving obligation. What does it cost you, after all? A little time and energy. Quite a bit less of both than it costs him to paint the ceiling, in fact.

And the odds are you'll get more orgasms out of it than he will doing the decorating. (Unless you're using a really funky kind of paint. In which case, please email me with the details immediately.)

A man who's getting regular sex will have a spring in his step. He'll fix the leaky tap that's been driving you mad without being asked four times. He'll take the kids out to ride their bikes and leave you in peace for an hour on Sunday afternoon, instead of slumping in front of Sky

Sports. He'll kiss you and rub your shoulders when he walks past, instead of ignoring you.

One hell of an investment on half an hour of bouncy-bouncy, if you ask me.

Honey v. vinegar

We've all got too used to dissing our husbands. These days, the natural assumption is that men are bastards and women suffer. And yes, in many parts of this book I've endorsed that view – because we've been looking at men who gave up on their marriages and looked elsewhere, and that still makes them cheating fuckers. Whilst there may be good reasons for having an affair, as we've been discussing, that still doesn't make it an excuse.

But right now we're not talking about *blame*. We're talking about how to *fix the problem.*

Ask yourself this: if knocking your man has become second nature to you, why are you still with him?

And if you do still love him, why don't you let yourself show it a little more often?

Women nag too much. We criticize all the time. (You know I'm right.) Girls, this is not the way to get what we want. You catch more flies with honey than vinegar, remember. Would you feel loved and appreciated if he bitched endlessly about the way you made the bed or folded his boxers?

Oh, but you only nag him because he ignores you otherwise, right?

Hate to be the one to break it to you, but men work and

think differently from women. If you ask him to take out the rubbish, he will; maybe only five minutes before the bin men arrive, but *he will do it.*

But what *you* mean when you ask him to take out the rubbish is *Take it out right now, so I can cross it off my list and move on to something else.*

He doesn't, so you ask him again. And he still doesn't, because he's in the middle of helping Johnny with his science project (at least, that's what he says the mess on the sitting-room carpet is all about), so this time you get kind of shrieky about it. He yells back and calls you a nag. So you slam out of the house, spilling the rubbish all down the driveway, and do it yourself.

How to get what you want, *not.*

If you want help, you have to accept that *his* way of doing things may not necessarily be *your* way, but that doesn't make it wrong. (Infuriating and pig-headed, yes, but not *wrong*.) My husband thinks he's better at laundry than me, because he puts stain remover along his collars before he washes them. I think I'm the professional because he never remembers to separate colours and whites and can't fold a T-shirt to save his life. Am I going to lose sleep arguing over it? What do you think?

Women want control, and then complain they're the ones left carrying the can. You're going to have to learn to let go a little. Or else do it all yourself and *stop bitching about it.*

The hill you wish to die on

Our mothers were so busy equipping us to take advantage

of all the opportunities they didn't have, they forgot to teach us how to compromise.

We're so used to fighting for our rights, to be taken seriously and treated equally, that we're terrified to give an inch or, God forbid, concede the most minor skirmish – even when the consequence is losing the entire war.

Do you really have to be right *all* the time? Can you let *nothing* go?

Or, as Dr Schlessinger puts it in her book *The Proper Care and Feeding of Husbands,* 'Is this the hill you wish to die on?'

Extraordinary how so many women are so brilliant at pinpointing the things their man does wrong, without ever turning that searing spotlight on themselves. Yes, it's annoying when he leaves his clothes on the floor. Yes, I wish he could get the coffee grounds *in* the bin. And, so help me God, if he uses my incredibly expensive Le Creuset saucepan to soak his paintbrushes in again, I'll kill him.

But are any of these nitpicking irritations deal breakers? Would you sacrifice your marriage for them?

Because in the end that's what it may come down to. Constant carping and criticism belittles and emasculates a man. He'll put up with a lot of nonsense and take pretty much everything you can throw at him . . . and then he won't.

And let's face it: our shit doesn't smell that sweet either.

Too many women kiss goodbye to their marriages and their husbands and a real shot at happiness because they've bought into the myth that women become *more* if they treat men as *less*.

Marriage is seen as a competition, a power struggle,

rather than a partnership. *I'm more tired/stressed/over-worked than you are. I do more around the house. I have less me-time. You have more freedom.*

Go toe-to-toe with each other and nobody wins (except those damn divorce lawyers).

So shake things up a little. Next time, try *agreeing* with him.

Him: 'Jesus, does it have to be total chaos when I get home? Is it too much to ask for a bit of peace and quiet? You've got no idea of the pressure I'm under at work—'

You: 'I'm sorry, I know you're tired. You've been working so hard lately. Look, why don't I put the kids to bed now and you can open a bottle of wine?'

Him (gobsmacked): 'No, it's OK. You've been stuck with the little blighters for the past two hours. I'll put them to bed. Tell you what, why don't I run you a bath? I'll even scrub your back if you like . . .'

The stamping of tiny feet

The one area where so many women refuse to compromise in a marriage isn't in the bedroom, or even the boardroom. An intelligent woman will accept that men have 'needs', and that if she wants to hold down a career and a marriage it often means taking on far more, and *doing* far more, than a man who wants the same two things.

No, the biggest marriage wrecker of all is the kids.

Women tend to put the children at the centre of the family, around whom all else revolves. Men want that centre to be them.

Many of the Infidels I spoke to in the course of researching this book had the same complaint:

'She's so wrapped up in the children,' one explained. 'She never has any time for me these days. Our sex life has more or less evaporated. What with her work and the kids, it's like she doesn't even know I'm there.'

10 things a man needs

1. To be a hero – to protect and rescue you (or at least think he does)
2. To be praised. Often and extravagantly
3. To care for and provide for you: recognize that his masculinity is wrapped up in his career
4. Appreciation – yes, a gold star and a thank you will go a long way
5. Sexual approval: show him you want to sleep with him and are satisfied when you do
6. To be the most important person in your life
7. For his opinions and decisions to be respected. Listen to him
8. For you to be interested in his day, his life, in him
9. A nurturing home life at which you, his wife and the mother of his children, are centre and present
10. Old-fashioned kindness and love

My ex-husband left three wives, each of them with children under the age of two. Three times, the birth of a child pushed him from the centre of the picture, and he was honest enough to admit he felt marginalized and shut out.

New fathers often feel excluded once children come

along. This usually has nothing to do with how they feel about the baby. But all the love and attention that was previously focused on them has suddenly been diverted to the squalling, red-faced scrap of flesh in their wife's arms. And men don't like taking second place in a woman's affections.

So they find a woman who puts them first.

> 'Childhood has been sanctified to such a degree that it no longer seems ridiculous for one adult to sacrifice herself entirely in order to foster the flawless and painless development of her offspring – a 24/7, one-person child-rearing factory.'
>
> **Esther Perel, *Mating in Captivity: Reconciling the Erotic and the Domestic***

My two siblings and I grew up in no doubt that we were loved, but also that we were of secondary importance in the family hierarchy.

My wise mother made it clear that, in our house, my father came first. 'He's the one I married,' she said. 'And he's the one I'll still be married to, long after you've all grown up and left home.'

In the evening, when my father got home, we were all sent out to play for thirty minutes so he didn't have to deal with our chaos straight from work. Brownies and Pony Club had to fit in around his golf or nights out at his club, never the other way round.

At the time, I thought my mother was downtrodden and old-fashioned, and couldn't imagine myself ever kowtowing to a man like that.

But her choices had nothing to do with giving up power or control. Only later, after my own divorce, did I understand it was about making sure my father knew he was the centre of her world.

Fifty years ago, children were seen as economic assets, sired to help with family income and to look after the parents in their old age. Today, they have no societal value other than to make us feel good. They rarely provide anything – in fact, they're an economic drain. Yet parents turn themselves inside-out to give their children the best chance of success, often at the expense of their own relationship.

On the shortlist of things that children actually require in order to thrive, parents with a loving relationship and healthy sex life should feature, too. It frees the child to do its own growing up and exploring in the world.

At some point, our over-indulged children are going to marry and have children of their own. If we don't teach them to put another person first they're going to be totally unequipped, not just for marriage, but also for parenthood.

Never had it so good

Relationships are tough. Actually, *life* is tough. Women still have to fight twice as hard, and be twice as good, to achieve the same recognition as a man in the workplace. We are usually still the ones who sacrifice our careers for the sake of our children. It's finally dawning on us that 'having it all' simply means *doing* it all.

Little wonder so many younger women are now hankering for a return to the lifestyle of a pre-war or 1950s housewife.

The Good Wife Guide (1939)

Marital Rating Scale: The Wife's Chart
George W. Crane, PhD, MD*

In computing the score, check the various items under Demerits which fit the wife, and add the total. Each item counts one point unless specifically weighted as in the parentheses. Then check items under Merits which apply; now subtract the Demerit score from the Merit score. The result is the wife's raw score.

Demerits

Slow in coming to bed, delays till husband is almost asleep

Doesn't like children (5)

Fails to sew on buttons or darn socks regularly

Wears soiled or ragged dresses and aprons around the house

Wears red nail polish

Often late for appointments (5)

Seams in hose often crooked

Goes to bed with curlers on or much face cream

Puts her cold feet on husband at night to warm them

Is a back seat driver

Flirts with other men at parties or in restaurants (5)

Is suspicious or jealous (5)

---

*From the *Journal of the American Psychological Association*

Merits

A good hostess – even to unexpected guests

Has meals on time

Can carry on interesting conversation

Can play a musical instrument e.g. piano, violin etc.

Dresses for breakfast

Neat housekeeper – tidy and clean

Personally puts children to bed

Never goes to bed angry, always makes up first (5)

Asks husband's opinions regarding important decisions and purchases

Good sense of humour – jolly and gay

Religious – sends children to church or Sunday school and goes herself (10)

Lets husband sleep late on Sundays and holidays

A recent survey for *New Woman* magazine revealed that 61 per cent of women with an average age of twenty-nine believe 'domestic goddess' role models who juggle top jobs with motherhood and jet-set social lives are 'unhelpful' and 'irritating'.

More than two-thirds thought a man should be the main provider in the family, whilst 70 per cent didn't want to work as hard as their mother's generation.

A quarter intended to give up work and be a full-time mother when they started a family (yes, I know; let's see how long that lasts once the true joy of cleaning up baby puke and wiping shitty bottoms 24/7 sinks in), whilst just 1 per cent said their career would remain a 'top priority' once they had kids.

What these women fail to realize is that the 1950s housewife put an awful lot back into her marriage and relationships in return for being 'kept'; not just in domestic labour, but in deferring to her husband – the 'main provider', remember – in a way modern women would find untenable.

Girls, we can't have it both ways.

If you want to duck out of the rat race and bake cookies with your babies, you have to accept that not only will you need to take on the bulk of the domestic chores, but your man will expect more from *you*. And, yes, likely he'll want to have the last word, too.

Life isn't a bed of roses for men these days either. They're under more pressure at work than ever before, competing with a far bigger workforce than their 1950s never-had-it-so-good counterparts, augmented as it has been by hundreds of thousands of successful, ambitious, intelligent women.

They're expected to be caring, sharing New Men; but to exhibit the same alpha-male hunter-gatherer traits women have found attractive since the dawn of time.

Frankly, they don't know what we want. Which isn't much of a surprise, since we don't know either.

Unclench your fist

The past fifty years have seen a seismic change in the nature of the relationship between men and women. We're all still coming to terms with the fall-out. Women's roles and expectations have altered dramatically, and men are even now struggling to catch up.

Maybe they *would* prefer it if we were more like our mothers (no, not literally; you know what I mean), though most of them have pretty much accepted that's never going to happen.

But that doesn't mean their most deep-seated needs and desires have changed. They still want the same things from a woman they always did. If we refuse to provide it, they'll simply go and find it elsewhere.

Women must stop thinking of our relationships as a competition. Instead of allowing ourselves to get caught up in our own problems, and fighting with him for airtime and attention, we need to remember we're on the same side. Lower the gun barrel. Cut him some slack. You'd be surprised how far a little *niceness* gets you. To paraphrase President Obama in his inauguration speech: your man will extend a hand if you are willing to unclench your fist.

An affair doesn't have to mean the end of your marriage. Whether or not you decide to stay with him is ultimately your choice.

Another woman can only come between you and your man *if you let her*.

Maybe you did take your eye off the ball for a split second. Maybe, in a moment of weakness, he did make a mistake. In that small space between you, the Bitch saw her opportunity and took it.

But it doesn't have to end there. If she threw a brick through your front window, would you go outside and hand her the keys to your house?

You can, and *should*, fight for what you want. If that includes your husband, then go out and take him back. Fight dirty. Play hard-ball. You know what to do now. Don't let some scheming little hussy destroy your life.

Beat the Bitch.

In a nutshell

- A good man won't look elsewhere unless you drive him to it
- Love isn't a feeling. It's a verb that requires effort and commitment
- You can't have it all. Something has to give
- It's official: men need sex
- Don't sweat the small stuff. Let it go
- Children are the product of your marriage, not its centre
- Compromise, compromise, compromise
- Beat the Bitch

Bibliography

Argov, Sherry *Why Men Love Bitches: From Doormat to Dreamgirl*, Adams Media, 2004

Dillner, Dr Luisa, *Love by Numbers: The Hidden Facts Behind Everyone's Relationships*, Profile Books, 2009

Farrell, Warren, *The Myth of Male Power*, Berkley Books, 1993

Houston, Ruth, *Is He Cheating on You? 829 Telltale Signs*, Lifestyle Publications, 2003

Landers, Elizabeth, and Mainzer, Vicky, *The Script: The 100 Per Cent Absolutely Predictable Things Men Do When They Cheat*, Hyperion, 2005

Lusterman, Don-David, *Infidelity – A Survival Guide*, New Harbinger Publications, 1998

Pittman, Frank, *Private Lies: Infidelity and the Betrayal of Intimacy*, Norton Books, 1989

Schlessinger, Dr Laura, *The Proper Care & Feeding of Husbands*, HarperCollins, 2004

Symonds, Sarah J., *Having an Affair?: A Handbook for the 'Other Woman'*, Red Brick Press, 2007

Staheli, Lana, *Affair-Proof Your Marriage*, Cliff Street Books, 1995

Vaughan, Peggy, *The Monogamy Myth*, Newmarket Press, 1989

Additional statistical sources

Blumstein and Schwartz, 1983

Date.com

Glass, Shirley B., and Wright, Thomas L., 'Justifications for Extramarital Relationships: the Association Between Attitudes, Behaviors, and Gender', *Journal of Sex Research*, Vol. 29, No. 3, August 1992

Halper, Jan, *Quiet Desperation*: The Truth About Successful Men, Warner Books, 1988

The Hite Report on Male Sexuality, 1972

Lifetime Cable Network

New Woman

New Scientist

Symantec

Do you have anything to add?
Visit Tess's website at

www.tessstimson.com

to contribute to the debate

Acknowledgements

How lucky am I, to have such a talented agent as Carole Blake, who has become one of my dearest friends; and such a smart, sassy and (thank heavens) patient editor as Lorraine Green, whose fishnet stockings and scarlet fuck-me shoes mean she'll probably never need this book.

Everyone at Blake Friedmann and Pan Macmillan – Oli Munson, Conrad Williams, my amazing PR Sandra Taylor, the infinitely patient Vicki Harris, Iram Allam, Shauna Bartlett, Ellen Wood, Tania Adams and Fiona Carpenter – you are bloody marvellous. You make my books stand out and take flight: seriously, I couldn't do any of this without you.

A special mention to Stephanie Sweeney, who first picked up on the idea for this book over champagne at supper, and woke up the next morning and still loved it. You're a total marvel. Thank you!

In researching this book, I spoke to dozens of men, both off and on the record, about their affairs; and to the women who were part of them, either as mistresses or betrayed wives and girlfriends. Thank you all for sharing your experiences so frankly and honestly. I have disguised names, locations and occupations in this book; any resemblance to anyone you think you know is purely coincidental.

Thanks, too, to Bel Mooney for her wise advice, and kindness in stopping to help a fellow journalist; and to my 'Deep Throats' in the legal profession, for their shrewd advice and insights into the world of divorce.

For this book almost more than any other, I've drawn on the common sense, wisdom and love of my mother, Jane, who died in December 2001, and whose loss I feel every single day. I miss you horribly.

To my ex-husband, Brent, and his wife, Jelena, who've walked with me every step of the way on this one: it's been a long road with a steep learning curve, but we got there. You're wonderful, and I love you both.

Kisses, too, to my father Michael and his wife, Barbi; to Sharon and Harry, Charles and Rachel, and to my own Dark Triad: Henry, Matthew and Lily. I love you all.

As always, the last word goes to Erik, my husband, who rarely if ever manages it in real life. You inspire me to do and be more, and I thank you from the bottom of my heart. You are just so damned easy to love.

Tess Stimson
Vermont, March 2009